# THE JOURNAL OF BEATLES STUDIES

Spring 2024

*The Journal of Beatles Studies*
Spring 2024

Cover image: Detail taken from Shutterstock, stock
photo ID 667520851. Photo contributor: Lenscap Photography.

ISBN (Paperback) 9781835532386
Online ISSN 2754-7019

**Publisher and Advertising**
Liverpool University Press, 4 Cambridge Street,
Liverpool, L69 7ZU (telephone: +44 (0)151-794 2233;
email: lup@liverpool.ac.uk;
web: www.liverpooluniversitypress.co.uk).
Full details of advertisement rates can be obtained
from the publisher.

To advertise in *The Journal of Beatles Studies*, contact
Natasha Bikkul, Journals Marketing Manager,
at nbikkul@liverpool.ac.uk.

*The Journal of Beatles Studies* is hosted online at
https://www.liverpooluniversitypress.co.uk/journal/jbs

**Identification Statement**
*The Journal of Beatles Studies* (online ISSN 2754-7019) is
published twice a year open access under a CC-BY licence
by Liverpool University Press, 4 Cambridge Street,
Liverpool, L69 7ZU.

*The Journal of Beatles Studies* is published in association
with the University of Liverpool.

**Open Access**
*The Journal of Beatles Studies* is a fully open access
journal and all content is freely available online.
All articles are published under a CC-BY licence.

Typeset by Carnegie Book Production, Lancaster.
Printed and bound by CPI Group (UK) Ltd, Croydon, CR0 4YY.

# Contents

| | |
|---|---|
| Contributors | 1 |
| Introduction<br>    *Holly Tessler and Paul Long* | 3 |

## Articles

| | |
|---|---|
| Echoes of the Beatles in Hamburg: the telling of the origin story<br>    *Hans Olof Gottfridsson* | 9 |
| Listen to what the man said: McCartney and journalistic objectivity — a test case<br>    *Martin Shough* | 35 |
| 'When Paul got an idea or an arrangement in his head...': inspiration, imagination, experimentation and transitions in 'Maxwell's Silver Hammer'<br>    *David Thurmaier* | 67 |
| Carry that weight: entrepreneurial teams, creativity and conflict in the Beatles<br>    *Nick Williams* | 87 |

## Across the Universe

| | |
|---|---|
| Thinking with the Beatles: on *Poppermost*<br>    *Andrew Wilson* | 113 |
| Poppermost<br>    *Pacôme Thiellement* | 127 |

# Reviews

*Blackbird: How Black Musicians Sang the Beatles into Being,* Katie Kapurch and Jon Marc Smith 139
    Gina Arnold

*Fashioning the Beatles: The Looks that Shook the World,* Deirdre Kelly 144
    Marlie Centawer

*Living the Beatles Legend: On the Road with the Fab Four — The Mal Evans Story,* Kenneth Womack 151
    Christian Lloyd

*The Beatles in Perspective: A Carnival of Light,* edited by James McGrath and Peter Mills 156
    Ben Winsworth

# Contributors

Hans Olof Gottfridsson, PhD, is a researcher at Karlstad University, Sweden. His main interest is the Beatles' early career and their time in Hamburg. His works include the book *The Beatles: From Cavern to Star Club*, which is the first complete account of the Beatles' recordings between 1957 and 1962. He has also contributed to a number of reissues of the Sheridan/Beatles recordings on disc, for which he was nominated for an American Grammy in 2013. Gottfridsson is the only outsider to have been given full access to the Star Club recordings with the Beatles.

Paul Long is co-editor of the *Journal of Beatles Studies* and Professor in Creative and Cultural Industries and director, Monash Migration and Inclusion Centre, Monash University, Melbourne, Australia.

Martin Shough studied photographic and print science at what is now the College of Communication, University of the Arts London. Books and articles on technical and anomalistic subjects include *A Social History of Ball Lightning* (Magonia 81(3) 2003/Darklore, 2014), *Double Trouble: The Science & Superstition of Multiple Suns* (Darklore, 2011), *Return to Magonia* (with Chris Aubeck, Anomalist Books, 2015) and *Redemption of the Damned* (with Wim van Utrecht, Anomalist Books, 2019 & 2021). He has been a photolithographer, semi-professional musician, artist and gallery owner. He lives in the north of Scotland.

Holly Tessler is co-editor of the *Journal of Beatles Studies* and Senior Lecturer in Music Industries and programme leader of the MA The Beatles, Music Industry and Heritage at the University of Liverpool, UK.

Pacôme Thiellement is the author of a stunningly eclectic body of work that includes 23 titles to date. His writing ranges between and among philosophy, film, television, music, poetry, the graphic novel and literature. His most recent publications include *Le Secret de la Société* (PUF, 2024) centered around the films of Jacques

Rivette, and *Déviations* (Éditions Anima, 2024) co-authored with the filmmaker Bertrand Mandico.

David Thurmaier is Associate Professor of Music Theory and director of graduate studies at the University of Missouri–Kansas City. His publications and presentations focus on the music of Charles Ives, the Beatles and music theory pedagogy. He co-hosts two music-related podcasts: 'I've Got a Beatles Podcast' and 'Hearing the Pulitzers'.

Nick Williams is Professor of Entrepreneurship at the University of Leeds. His research focuses on entrepreneurship and economic development, as well as dynamics and conflict in entrepreneurial teams.

Andrew Wilson is a graduate of the Master of Philosophy Programme in Literary Translation at Trinity College Dublin. He has taught at State University of New York at Buffalo and L'Institut Charles V (Paris). He is currently affiliated with the Centre for Literary Translation at Trinity College Dublin as a creative practitioner. His published translations include the works of Sébastien Brebel, Bruce Bégout and Antoine Volodine. He is currently working on a translation of Olivier Bruneau's sf novel *Esther*.

# Introduction

On 20 February 2024 Sony Pictures Entertainment announced that director Sam Mendes plans to tell the story of the Beatles in film, a project that has the blessing and cooperation of Apple Corps. The approach is ambitious in scope and scale, the intention to create a cinematic event. As Mendes commented: 'I'm honored to be telling the story of the greatest rock band of all time, and excited to challenge the notion of what constitutes a trip to the movies.' Aiming for theatrical release in 2027, the story is to be told through four separate films, each directed by Mendes and focused individually on the perspective of either Paul McCartney, John Lennon, George Harrison or Ringo Starr (Sony Pictures 2024).

New projects across media forms such as these planned films attest to the ongoing appetite for the music of the Beatles, for knowledge about their lives and their impact as a cultural force. New projects suggest that the audience for the Beatles is potentially infinite, comprising those who were there at the beginning as well as new generations who share in creating innovative communities of interest and forms of fandom. The global reach of the Beatles audiences, new and old, and their receptiveness to new material indicates both the continuing cultural weight of the band as well as their economic value. After all, to commit to four films represents a considerable investment for which Sony will expect significant return. Their appearance will no doubt amplify a demand for the Beatles' musical catalogue, underpinning the approval of Apple, which diligently manages the band's legacy and financial portfolio.

One need not be a dedicated fan to encounter the Beatles' music and related events as they regularly continue to make news in this way. Since the last issue of the *Journal of Beatles Studies*, for instance, we have welcomed (though some lamented) the release of 'Now and Then', pointedly labelled by Apple as 'the last Beatles song'. Created from a 1970s Lennon demo, the song was tried out in the sessions for the *Anthology* series in 1995 that produced 'Free as a Bird' and 'Real Love'. Rejected at the time for its lack of sound quality, the 'new' version can claim (for the moment) to be *The End*, as it features original performances by all four Beatles. With added poignancy, the song was released on vinyl paired with 'Love Me Do', which was 'de-mixed using machine aided learning and remixed in true stereo' (thesoundofvinyl.com).

The promotional value of this release served the 50th anniversary of the 1973 compilation sets *1962–1966* and *1967–1970*. Popularly known as the 'red' and 'blue' double albums respectively, these collections now fill six vinyl discs and offer a total of 75 songs – 21 more than the original package. While this material has long been available, 36 of the recordings have been remixed and the discs come with generous sleeve notes courtesy of British journalist John Harris. This generosity, like Mendes' planned film quartet, is a notable aspect of the economy of creativity and attention produced by and devoted to the Beatles. 'Now and Then' was in part made possible thanks to technologies and techniques developed for Peter Jackson's *The Beatles: Get Back* (2021). Famously, that documentary series reworked the 81 minutes of Michael Lindsay-Hogg's *Let It Be* (1970), building 7 hours and 48 minutes of TV from nearly 60 hours of film footage and 150 hours of audio. Reviewed in this issue, Ken Womack's *Living the Beatles Legend: The Untold Story of Mal Evans* (2023), a biography of the band's roadie and general dogsbody, is told in nearly 600 pages. On his website, Beatles historian Mark Lewisohn acknowledges that 'I appreciate that people hungrily want my next book NOW. Thank you.' *Tune In*, the first of a projected trilogy, *The Beatles: All These Years*, took ten years to research and was published in 2013, with no date yet set for volume 2, let alone the final volume. That first book ran to 1728 pages in a special edition expanding on the mere 960 of the 'ordinary' version.

At its best, the variety and extent of this kind of material signposts a regard for the significance of the Beatles, offering expansive empirical detail and new insights, if not always sharp analysis or argument. Certainly, *Get Back*'s scenes of creativity and camaraderie, among those depicting undoubted tensions, has impacted on the rather two-dimensional account of the band's break-up. Lewisohn's approach to relating an account of the Beatles' emergence without recourse to a sense of inevitable success is described as 'anti-myth' (marklewisohn.net). While myths may have their appeal, they also tend to authorize hagiography and hyperbole, demanding repetition while, potentially, limiting understanding and debate. A regular challenge for the editors and peer reviewers supporting this journal is to prompt some authors of research articles submitted for consideration to be reflexive about such tendencies and about recourse to ready-made templates for narrating Beatles histories and interpretations.

Elsewhere, like others researching Beatles history, meanings and cultural economies, the editors of this journal are flattered to find themselves sometimes called upon to add our expert commentary to media news items. The framing of reports itself tells us much about how the band is narrated and how it lends itself to the narrative of other artists and events. For instance, Taylor Swift's *Eras* tour reached Australia in February 2024, incidentally the year that marks six decades since the Beatles toured the country, generating record crowds *outside* of concert venues. Sustained excitement and attention surrounded Swift in terms of the rapid sale of tickets, the size of her concert audiences and indeed their devotion. One question, in a variety of permutations, was repeatedly posed by media presenters, who asked: 'Are we witnessing a new Beatlemania?' Invitations such as this might invite hyperbolic responses, although it is possible to interrogate why and how it might be useful to measure contemporary musical stardom with reference to the moment of the Beatles. Swift's success and recent elevation as a potential threat to some on the right of the political spectrum in the United States certainly makes for interesting discussion, for instance in terms of the patronizing take on her female fans. Disdain for young fans certainly echoes what Christine Feldman-Barrett has written about in her *Women's History of the Beatles* (2021). In light of quizzical and hostile responses from some to the idea of Beatles Studies, we are particularly sympathetic to those who wish to treat Taylor Swift as an object of cultural significance or research who find their enterprises scrutinized (Spurrier 2024).

Ultimately, the generation of new material and original prompts to narrating the Beatles, using them and their music as an explanatory lens, sustains the objectives of this journal to produce original research. We are pleased then to present new articles that interrogate some familiar and often shop-worn reference points, as well as introducing original perspectives on the Beatles from a non-Anglophone context.

Hans Olof Gottfridsson addresses the much mythologized 'Hamburg period' of the Beatles' history. In 'Echoes of the Beatles in Hamburg: the original story as it was told in the 1960s' he examines sources from the 1960s for reportage on and the emergence and development of what he calls 'the original Liverpool narrative', 'the media narrative' and an official 'Beatles narrative', examining the influence of these frames for how we think of that moment. In a similar vein, Martin Shough examines how the contemporary press has treated Paul McCartney's recollections of how the Beatles became politically conscious in the 1960s, particularly with reference to protests against the American war in Vietnam. 'Listen to what the man said: McCartney and journalistic objectivity — a test case' is an example of the rigorous, original and revisionist 'citizen scholarship' that we introduced in the last issue, one that builds a convincing argument on exhaustive historical work. David Thurmaier offers new perspectives on one of the Beatles' most maligned recordings, 'Maxwell's Silver Hammer'. Examining a host of rehearsal tapes, the song is scrutinized and indeed appreciated for its inspiration, imagination and experimentation in the context of the unravelling of the band's creative and productive working relationship. Thurmaier's study has some crossover with 'Carry that weight' in which Nick Williams examines 'entrepreneurial teams, creativity and conflict in the Beatles'. Building on the theory of entrepreneurial teams to review some familiar narratives of the Beatles' rise and fall, Williams examines the role of leadership in underpinning the creativity and cohesion of the band, tracing the loss of these qualities after the death of Brian Epstein, and making good use of *The Beatles: Get Back* as a primary source.

Framed in the context of our *Across the Universe* section, Andrew Wilson provides an introduction to the work and ideas of French cultural theorist and commentator Pacôme Thiellement. This is a preface to a translation from the French of a key chapter from Thiellement's book of 2002, *Poppermost: Considérations sur la mort de Paul McCartney* [Poppermost: Thoughts on the Death of Paul McCartney]. Wilson offers a precis of Thiellement's understanding of the Beatles and popular music more generally that relates his thought to broader theoretical traditions. For Anglophone cultural scholars unfamiliar with this work, it offers interesting points of comparison for treating the Beatles and pop as a meaningful form. Importantly, Wilson gives us insight into one tradition representative of our general invitation to scholars from beyond the English-speaking worlds to relate local perspectives, experiences and meanings of the Beatles.

Our book reviews continue to survey the productive and broad field of Beatles scholarship, which is by no means captured and contained in our limited pages. Here, Gina Arnold reviews *Blackbird: How Black Musicians Sang the Beatles into Being* by Katie Kapurch and Jon Marc Smith, an important new work that examines the band's relationship with black music, Marlie Centawer considers Deirdre Kelly's *Fashioning the Beatles*, and Christian Lloyd reports on the aforementioned *Living the Beatles Legend: The Untold Story of Mal Evans* by Kenneth Womack. Finally, Ben Winsworth reads James McGrath and Peter Mills's edited collection *The Beatles in Perspective: A Carnival of Light*.

We continue to invite original research that speaks to our desire to extend the space of thinking about and with the Beatles, testing our premises, the research we publish here and this wider sphere of investigation and debate.

Holly Tessler
*University of Liverpool, UK*
*Holly.Tessler@liverpool.ac.uk*

Paul Long
*Monash University, Australia*
*paul.long@monash.edu*

Co-editors, the *Journal of Beatles Studies*

## Bibliography

Feldman-Barrett, C. (2021) *A Women's History of the Beatles* (New York: Bloomsbury Publishing USA).

Lewisohn, M. (2013) *The Beatles: All These Years – Extended Special Edition: Volume One: Tune In* (London: Hachette).

Sony Pictures (2024) 'Sam Mendes/Neal Street Productions to make landmark Beatles biopic project for Sony Pictures Entertainment', press release, 20 February, https://www.sonypictures.com/corp/press_releases/2024/0220 (accessed 20 February 2024).

https://thesoundofvinyl.com.au/collections/the-beatles/products/the-beatles-now-and-then-blue-7 (accessed 20 February 2024).

Spurrier, K. (2024) 'As the V&A advertises for a "Taylor Swift Super Fan Adviser", an Oxford graduate who wrote a dissertation on the singer provocatively claims she is as culturally important as Shakespeare, Chaucer and Wordsworth', *Mail Online*, 25 February, https://www.dailymail.co.uk/tvshowbiz/article-13121459/museum-Taylor-Swift-fan-Oxford-graduate-singer-Shakespeare-Chaucer-Wordsworth.html (accessed 25 February 2024).

Womack, K. (2023) *Living the Beatles Legend: The Untold Story of Mal Evans* (New York: Dey Street Books).

# Echoes of the Beatles in Hamburg
## The telling of the origin story

Hans Olof Gottfridsson
*University of Karlstad, Department of Geography, Media and Communication, SE-651 88 Karlstad, Sweden*
*hans.olof.gottfridsson@kau.se*

**Abstract:** The Beatles' Hamburg period is important for the group's early career in particular, and is among the most rewritten periods, not least after the group split in 1970. The aim of this article is to identify the original British Hamburg narrative from the 1960s, both its sources and changes in the stories during the decade. For this purpose, a broad review has been made of existing media material from the period. The result shows the existence of extensive 1960s source material and several contemporary narratives of the period, divided here into three categories: the 'Liverpool narrative', the 'national narrative' and the 'official narratives'. The most primary is the Liverpool material; the most diverse is the national material; and the one with the greatest impact both in the 1960s and later is the official publications.

**Keywords:** the Beatles, Hamburg, Star Club, Kaiserkeller, Indra Club, Top Ten Club

The Beatles' time in Hamburg was given, from the very beginning, while the band was still playing there, great importance for their development into a top act (*Mersey Beat* 1961c: 5). The importance of the Hamburg era for the band also recurs, as will become clear later, in both the group's own stories and media reporting during the 1960s, and the period is given central importance in many later publications about the group as well (e.g., Gottfridsson 1997; Lewisohn 2013; Knublauch 2021).

> Sure WE [the Beatles] come from Liverpool. There are hundreds of groups there, many on an R and B kick. But you won't hear us shouting around about a Liverpool Sound, or Merseybeat, simply because it's been dreamed up as an easy way to describe what's going on with our music, 'Hamburg stamp and Yell' music might be more accurate, It was all chat work on various club stages in Germany that built up our beat. (George Harrison in *Beatles Book* 1964: 23)

This article traces the original story of the Beatles' Hamburg period in the British media between 1960 and 1969. The intention is to make a complete review of the existing material in the field and to identify the origin of the original stories. The aim is also to see connections between different sources and changes in the stories during the decade. However, there is no ambition to establish the degree of historical truth in the stories, to create a biography of the Beatles' Hamburg period, or to explain the origin of events.

Narrative storytelling can be described as using the narrative form as a tool to study and structure the past. There are several principles for this, one of which is a division between chronological-based narratives and structure/discourse-based narratives. However, arguments can be made that both of these perspectives are required for understanding and can be used together (Puckett 2016). This means that the source material on the Beatles' Hamburg era is presented here in the form of a structure/discourse-based narrative where the material has been divided into three categories: the 'Liverpool narrative', the 'national narrative' and the 'official narratives'. This division is based on the content, origin and context of the source material and is further defined later in the article. The material is also categorized and interpreted from a chronological perspective, where the material is presented in order of publication and analysed based on the extent or otherwise of a chronologically coherent storyline. Stories are also a product of context, and narratives change continuously depending on time and circumstances (Puckett 2016). So, too, does the Beatles' Hamburg narrative, and, as initially stated, this article also aims to identify the changes in the stories told during the decade.

This article is based on a complete review of British media material from the 1960s with references to the Beatles' Hamburg era, such as newspapers, magazines, books and interview material from press conferences, television and radio. The fact that media material about the Beatles is extensive and not fully available through public archives or digital sources has in turn made the collection and analysis a time-consuming part of the work on this article.

## The Liverpool narrative

The 'Liverpool narrative' is based on local Liverpool media, main sources being the entertainment magazine *Mersey Beat* and the daily *Liverpool Echo*. The source material in *Mersey Beat* is extensive, a total of over twenty features between 1961 and 1963, making it the publication that wrote about the subject on the greatest number of occasions during the 1960s. The features in the *Liverpool Echo* are fewer, but they were the first in which a wider audience could read about the group and their connection to Hamburg.

### *Pre-fame reporting between 1961 and 1962*

The first public account of the Beatles' time in Hamburg can be found in the first issue of *Mersey Beat*, published in early July 1961, just days after the group had returned from the second of a total of five stints in Hamburg between 1960 and 1962. The source is the John Lennon-penned text 'Being a Short Diversion on the Dubious Origins of the Beatles', which elaborates on the reasons for the band's residency. According to Lennon's version of events, the background to the first contract to play in Hamburg in 1960 was that 'a man [Allan Williams] with a beard cut off said—will you go to Germany [Hamburg] and play mighty rock for the peasants for money? And we said we would play mighty anything for money' (*Mersey Beat* 1961a: 2). In the piece, Lennon also gives, albeit in a sheepishly goonish way, a first set of foundations for the future Hamburg narrative. Here, beside recounting the origin of the Hamburg contract, he also describes how Pete Best joined the band for the Hamburg trip, the fire at the Bambi-Filmkunstheater/ Bambi Kino [Bambi Film Art Theatre/Bambi Cinema], the expulsion of Paul McCartney and Best, and how George Harrison was sent home because he was a minor. His article ends with the Beatles returning from Hamburg having originated a musical identity with a new style of their own, performing at various clubs in Liverpool for a period before returning to Hamburg for a second visit (*Mersey Beat* 1961a: 2).

In the second issue of *Mersey Beat*, another basic feature of the Hamburg story was given: the recordings the Beatles made with Tony Sheridan. This time the story featured as front-page news (*Mersey Beat* 1961b: 1). During the autumn of 1961 *Mersey Beat* continued to report on the release and availability of the Hamburg recordings. At the end of November, the paper reported how Brian Epstein, prompted by inquiries in his record shop, directly imported the single 'My Bonnie' from Germany (*Mersey Beat* 1961d: 6). Later, the magazine also recounted how, with Epstein's help, this record was released in the UK in January 1962 (*Mersey Beat* 1961–62a: 4). Along with *Melody Maker*, *Mersey Beat* also reported that the Beatles had carried out a second recording session with Sheridan in Hamburg in the spring of 1962, when they recorded 'Swany' [Swanee River] and 'Sweet Georgia Brown' (*Mersey Beat* 1962e: 7; *Melody Maker* 1962b: 2). *Mersey Beat* was also the only British source that noted the release in Germany of the LP *My Bonnie* (*Mersey Beat* 1962c: 9).

Another of the future cornerstones of the Hamburg story can be found in the *Mersey Beat* of August 1961, where Cavern DJ Bob Wooler, in his column in the paper, was the first writer to refer to Hamburg as the place where the Beatles underwent a transformation to return to Liverpool as a top act (*Mersey Beat* 1961c: 5). This is a mantra that would be consistently repeated in future reporting about the Beatles' time in Hamburg.

In December 1961 *Mersey Beat* wrote again about the Beatles and Hamburg, this time as part of a biography of Derry and the

Seniors, the first Liverpool band to go to Germany. In the article, Howie Casey, a member of the band, praised the Beatles, who shared the stage with them in Hamburg in 1960. Casey also recalls 'the kingsize cock-up when it was arranged for us [Derry and the Seniors] to do a season at Blackpool, and so like Greenhorns, we all turned pro, and then nothing came of it!' (*Mersey Beat* 1961—62b: 4). The comment lacks context but is a preface to the narrative, and refers to a cancelled tour that ultimately led to the band and Williams travelling to London in search of work. There they met the German club owner Bruno Koschmider and got a contract to play the Kaiserkeller in Hamburg. This story would not become widely known until the publication of Hunter Davies' official biography of the band, *The Beatles*, in 1968.

During 1962 *Mersey Beat* continued its reporting on the Beatles' activities in Hamburg, now in real time as events happened. The focus was on their ongoing gigs at the Star Club, but also events such as Stuart Sutcliffe's sudden death in Germany (e.g., *Mersey Beat* 1962c: 8; 1962b: 4; 1962d: 8). The magazine also noted that Ringo Starr, not yet a member of the Beatles in early 1962, had joined Sheridan at the Top Ten Club in Hamburg (*Mersey Beat* 1962a: 4).

In August 1961, the local daily the *Liverpool Echo* picked up a story from *Mersey Beat* regarding how Paul McCartney had lost the address of a girl in a hospital in Liverpool to whom he had promised to bring a doll from Germany, and added that he had spent three months in Germany with a group from Liverpool, the Beatles (*Mersey Beat* 1961e: 4; *Liverpool Echo* 1961: 3). This was the first time, albeit in a very brief piece, that a wider audience was able to read about the Beatles and their residency in Hamburg. The *Liverpool Echo* continued to write about the band's Hamburg connection during 1962; in January, in conjunction with the UK release of 'My Bonnie' (*Liverpool Echo* 1962a: 16; 1962b: 17), and again in May, linked to the news that the group had secured an audition for Parlophone (*Liverpool Echo* 1962d: 6). The *Liverpool Echo* also mentioned the Hamburg connection when reporting the death of Sutcliffe in April 1962, but without mentioning the group by name (*Liverpool Echo* 1962c: 10).

### Reporting after the national breakthrough from 1963 and onwards

Between April and September 1963 *Mersey Beat* published an eleven-part series of articles on the Beatles' early career, the first of its kind. Although the articles do not form a coherent narrative but are rather a series of independent interviews and reflections without direct connection to each other, they provide the embryo for the first more complete Hamburg narrative and comprise well over 1,500 words on the subject. Here, Allan Williams gives his version of how the first Hamburg contract came about, how Best was hired for the Hamburg job, and how he himself took the Beatles to Hamburg in his minibus. The tough living conditions in Hamburg are also described, as are the many hours on stage and how the demanding German audience quickly forced the Beatles to broaden their repertoire and develop their stage act. The series also includes McCartney and Best's first testimony about the fire incident at the Bambi Cinema and their expulsion from Hamburg in December 1960. The recordings with Sheridan are also highlighted, as is 'My 'Bonnie' as the reason why Epstein discovered the band and became their manager. Also included are Casey's personal memories of both playing with Sutcliffe and sharing the stage with the Beatles in Hamburg. Among Casey's memories are those telling of how the Seniors and the Beatles, in order to get a new and better stage at the Kaiserkeller, together destroyed the old one. This story would also be retold later in the 1960s in alternative versions by both Best and the Beatles (see *Beatles Book* 1963–64/ Shepherd 1964; *TeenSet* 1965: 44–48; Davies 1968). Finally, the *Mersey Beat* series also featured Rory Storm and the Hurricanes member Lu Walter's recollections of his time in Hamburg with Ringo Starr (*Mersey Beat* 1963a).

After mid-1963 the number of Beatles and Hamburg features in *Mersey Beat* decreased considerably. However, there are two later features in the paper worth mentioning, as they are exclusive to the Liverpool narrative. The first is about a private recording made by Lennon, McCartney and Harrison with the aforementioned Walters and Ringo Starr in Hamburg in October 1960, which was financed by Williams and whose existence is otherwise only briefly mentioned in a by-line in the *Disc and Music Echo* (*Mersey Beat*

1963—64: 17; *Disc and Music Echo* 1966: 2). The other is a colour photograph of the Beatles live at the Star Club in 1962, part of a set of photos commissioned by Bill Harry, founder and editor of *Mersey Beat*, and published exclusively in the magazine in March 1964 (*Mersey Beat* 1964: 1).

As a final aspect of this framing period, it can be highlighted that the reporting in *Mersey Beat* not only focused on the Beatles and their time in Hamburg but also on other Liverpool bands playing there, and artists such as, for instance, Kingsize Taylor and Lee Curtis, who were both more successful in Hamburg than the Beatles and came to have the major part of their careers in Germany (e.g., *Mersey Beat* 1962f: 9; Krüger 2010). Also in focus was the strong musical bond that developed over time between Liverpool and Hamburg, or, as the magazine later called the city, 'the other Merseyside' (*Mersey Beat* 1963f: 9).

As the first source for the Hamburg era, the Liverpool narrative provides the basic elements of the story. However, although the initial summary of the Beatles' career can be found here, this narrative lacks a coherent storyline. Furthermore, its impact was limited outside Merseyside and Northern England during the 1960s.

## The national narrative

The 'national narrative' is based on the British pop and teenage press and interview material from press conferences, television and radio. The latter material is limited in scope, while the press material is much more extensive, consisting of nearly fifty different features spread across more than twenty different magazines, with most published between 1963 and 1964. The main source is *NME*, which, together with *Melody Maker*, contains just over a third of all articles from the period.

The source material for the national narrative lacks a coherent form. Here, to improve clarity, the material has been organized by content.

## The narrative in the press before 'Love Me Do'

All the writing about the Beatles in the national British pop and teen press before the release of 'Love Me Do' in October 1962 is about the Hamburg recordings. The earliest features comprise a number of reviews of the UK release of the single 'My Bonnie/The Saints' from early January 1962 (*NME* 1962a: 4; *Melody Maker* 1962a: 11; *Disc* 1962a: 9). To these can be added a review of 'My Bonnie' in the Gloucestershire-based weekly the *Tewkesbury Register* (*Tewkesbury Register* 1962: 3). Another early reference to the Hamburg recordings is a brief mention in *Melody Maker* in August 1962 that the Beatles, or 'Beaties' as the magazine called them, had recorded 'Swanee River' with Sheridan for German Polydor (*Melody Maker* 1962b: 2). This event was also noted in *Mersey Beat* (*Mersey Beat* 1962e: 7).

The British pop press continued to give the Hamburg recordings space after 1962, mainly in connection with the release of both new records and reissues of old material that followed in 1963–64 in the wake of the Beatles' success (e.g., *NME* 1964c: 6; *Melody Maker* 1964: 1). However, while record releases were a frequent topic in the British pop press in the early 1960s, the nature of the recordings themselves was never touched upon in any detail. Most informative is an interview with Sheridan in *Disc* and one with him and German music publishing executive Alfred Schacht in *Fabulous*, both from 1964. However, even these sources are sketchy in their details of what was recorded and where and when these recording sessions took place (*Disc* 1964: 2; *Fabulous* 1964: 8–9). Also notable from press material is that although the Hamburg recordings were high on the sales charts in many countries during the 1960s, both the Beatles and Sheridan were quick to express a clear distaste for them in the press (e.g., *Melody Maker* 1963a: 1; *Combo* 1964: 3; *Cashbox* 1964: 28). In addition, one can add to this ambivalence the critical discussions in the British pop press in the 1960s about how damaging the re-release of the Hamburg recordings was to the Beatles' contemporary career (*New Record Mirror* 1963b: 3; 1964: 11).

In summary, the Hamburg recordings are the single subject that the press wrote about most during the 1960s. It can also be noted that during this decade these recordings were released on disc in a large number of versions and variants worldwide, not only in the UK, and today they are among the most reissued recordings of all categories (Gottfridsson 2001).

## The narrative in the press after 'Love Me Do'

It was only after the release of 'Love Me Do' that the national British pop and teen press began to pay attention to the Beatles as a band. During the autumn of 1962 several articles about them were published, many with reference to their ongoing engagement in Hamburg, but also their history in the city (*NME* 1962b: 2; 1962c: 6; *New Record Mirror* 1962: 6; *Disc* 1962b: 4). At the same time, trade papers such as *The Stage and Television Today* and EMI's *Record Mail* also picked up the story, with the latter being the first at the national level to give a more detailed account of the group's time in Hamburg and the recordings made there with Sheridan (*The Stage and Television Today* 1962: 7; *Record Mail* 1962: 6). Several self-produced advertisements can also be located in the pop press towards the end of 1962, in which the band sent seasonal greetings from Hamburg to their supporters in the UK. An example can be found in *Pop Weekly* (*Pop Weekly* 1962: 17).

The first national British pop magazine to report in depth on the emerging British music scene in Hamburg and the Beatles' time in the city was *New Record Mirror*. In March 1963 it sent a reporter to Hamburg to interview Peter Eckhorn, owner of the Top Ten Club, and Iain Hines, one of the British Hamburg rock 'n' roll pioneers and then manager of the same club. The article addressed the fact that the Top Ten Club had become a hot spot for British bands, but it was also the first, apart from Lennon's article in *Mersey Beat*, to tell the story of the fire at the Bambi Cinema and the subsequent expulsion of McCartney and Best. It was also the first to tell how the Beatles, thanks to Eckhorn, were later able to return to Hamburg, and that 'My Bonnie' had so far sold 100,000 copies in Germany (*New Record Mirror* 1963a: 2). Eckhorn was interviewed again just over a year later by the same reporter in *Record Mirror*, this time in London. New information this time included Eckhorn's account of how he travelled to Liverpool in late December 1961 and hired Ringo Starr as Sheridan's drummer, an event already noted in *Mersey Beat* in January 1962. He also recounted how, during the same visit, he reunited with the Beatles and met their new manager, Brian Epstein, for the first time (*Record Mirror* 1964: 8—9; *Mersey Beat* 1962a: 4).

*Record Mirror* was not alone in sending reporters to Hamburg during the 1960s. *Fabulous* and *NME* also interviewed Manfred Weissleder, the owner of the Star Club. In *Fabulous*, in 1964, Weissleder told the story of how the Beatles, whom he described as lively boys, borrowed a car from him to go to the seaside, which they then wrecked and abandoned. He also claimed, contrary to many others, that the Beatles were never poorly paid in Hamburg, especially not at the Star Club (*Fabulous* 1964: 8—9). In *NME*, in 1966, Weissleder recalled how the Beatles destroyed his car and told of how Lennon performed at the Star Club with a toilet seat around his neck, the latter a story that had already been recounted in 1964 by Horst Fascher, a friend of the Beatles and an employee of the clubs they played at in Hamburg (*Beatles Book* 1963—64/Shepherd 1964). Weissleder's narrative also includes an account of how, when he saw the Beatles for the first time, long before he hired them, he perceived them as visitors from another planet. Moreover, he talked about how Lennon and Little Richard used to argue with each other constantly, but also how the latter predicted that the Beatles could become the biggest act in the whole world. The stories also included how Epstein, when he demanded higher wages from Weissleder, used the argument that the Beatles would one day be bigger than Elvis (*NME* 1966: 3). The *NME* article, written at the same time as the Beatles' return to Hamburg in June 1966, also recounts how old friends from the early years in the city visited the band backstage between their performances, and how Astrid Kirchherr then returned a number of letters to Lennon that he had written to Sutcliffe in Hamburg. *Fabulous* in turn contained, in addition to the interview with Weissleder, others with Hines, Sheridan and Schacht. Also memorable from *Fabulous* is that the Beatles feature ends with a twist, in which the journalist who wrote the piece orders a Beatles dish — a chocolate drink in a bottle, long, fat curry sausages, and yellow chips — from the same woman who once used to serve this menu to the band (*Fabulous* 1964: 8—9).

Sheridan's importance as a mentor to the Beatles in Hamburg was already established in 1963 in *Mersey Beat* (*Mersey Beat* 1963d: 2; 1963f: 9). By contrast, his own accounts of his time with the Beatles in Hamburg were limited across the wider 1960s, and in the interviews that he did give to the press he was usually more interested in promoting his own ongoing career than sharing old memories of the Beatles (e.g., *Combo* 1964: 3). Examples of press material in which Sheridan does address his time with the Beatles in Hamburg are the aforementioned interview in *Disc* and a shorter interview in *Fabulous* (*Disc* 1964: 6; *Fabulous* 1964: 8—9). Most informative, however, is an article in *NME* from March 1964 in which he described his time with the Beatles in Hamburg: a rave from morning to night, long hours on stage, poor accommodation and frequent visits to the British Seamen's Mission for tea and breakfast cereal. Standing out in Sheridan's *NME* story is a violent fist fight outside the Top Ten Club between him and Best, which ended, however, in reconciliation (*NME* 1964b: 7). This obviously had some impact on both combatants, as it was also recounted by Best in various contexts during the 1960s (e.g., *TeenSet* 1965: 44—48; Davies 1968). In the *NME* report, it can also be read that Sheridan claimed at the time to have recorded a joint composition by him and McCartney from the Hamburg era, 'Tell Me if You Can' (*NME* 1964b: 7). This was a recording that the paper had already listed as Sheridan's next single release the month before, but which never materialized (*NME* 1964a: 10).

The wider public first knew of Astrid Kirchherr's connection with the Beatles through Shepherd in late 1963 (*Beatles Book* 1963—64/ Shepherd 1964). Her own media debut was in the German tabloid *Bild-Zeitung* in February 1964 (*Bild-Zeitung* 1964: 5). Six months later she was interviewed in British *Rave* and American *Motion Picture* (*Rave* 1964: 19—24; *Motion Picture* 1964: 1—5). All of these articles, which offer the first building blocks in the legend of the great love story between her and Sutcliffe and their importance to the Beatles, are largely similar in character and content. They are about the couple's first meeting at the Kaiserkeller, their love affair, Kirchherr's photographs of the band, Sutcliffe's ambition to be a painter rather than a rock star, his early death, and Kirchherr as the grieving girlfriend. Unlike *Bild-Zeitung* and *Motion Picture*, however, *Rave* does not acknowledge Kirchherr as the creator of the Beatles' hairstyles, nor Sutcliffe as an original Beatle. Also specific to *Rave* is the almost excruciatingly detailed description of Sutcliffe's illness and death, a subject that is admittedly also a main focus in the other two articles but not dealt with in such detail (*Rave* 1964: 19—24).

To the material on Sutcliffe from the 1960s can be added a biography of him published in September 1968. The article, published in the *Observer*, contains the first comprehensive account of his life and work and includes contributions from, among others, his mother, Millie Sutcliffe, Liverpool friend Rod Murray, and his teacher at the Hamburg College of Art, Eduardo Paolozzi (*Observer* 1968: 23—24).

In the 1960s Iain Hines was one of the most frequent commentators on the Beatles' time in Hamburg (e.g., *New Record Mirror* 1963a: 2; *Fabulous* 1964: 8—9; *16 Magazine* 1965: 9—12; *Beatles Book* 1966a). In the spring of 1966 he appeared in a series of articles about British beat bands in Hamburg in *Beat Instrumental* (*Beat Instrumental* 1966). In these articles he once again recounted, among other things, his memories of the Beatles' expulsion from Germany in the winter of 1960. What was new was that he breathed new life into the story of how he, Sheridan and the Jets were the first British rock band to travel to Hamburg, thus paving the way for the Beatles and other bands. The *Record and Show Mirror* had written about this as early as November 1960, but with the dominance of Liverpool bands in the early 1960s it had faded from the media reporting by the mid-60s (*Beat Instrumental* 1966: 18; *Record and Show Mirror* 1960: 17).

In passing, it can be noted that the Beatles' own statements about Hamburg in the British pop and teen press during the 1960s are relatively few and that it is instead mainly in the official material that their accounts can be found. Worth noting from the press material, however, is a feature in *Melody Maker* from August 1963, where the band for the first time in the national press addressed the importance of the Hamburg era (*Melody Maker* 1963b: 6—7). Also interesting is a comment by Lennon in *NME*, in July 1966, where he claims that they were framed by the owner of the Kaiserkeller for the fire at the Bambi Cinema (*NME* 1966: 3). A comment by Harrison two years later in the same paper can also be added, where he says that the group at that moment were working to become as musically tight as when they were on stage in Hamburg and at the Cavern (*NME* 1968: 3). This statement heralded the 'Get Back' project of the following January, through which the band sought to return to the basics of their music-making. Finally, there is McCartney's now largely forgotten story, also from *NME*, about how the band were, to their dismay, served fish and horseradish sauce for Christmas dinner by good friends in Hamburg in 1962 (*NME* 1963: 3).

In the case of ex-Beatle Pete Best, his narrative of the Hamburg era was presented primarily in the American press, and between mid-1964 and the summer of 1966 he contributed to nearly ten different American youth magazines. Most of these stories later reappeared in Davies' biography of the band, but never in the British press (Davies 1968).

In conclusion, what characterizes the national narrative after 'Love Me Do' is the many individual stories, which are often detailed, not infrequently with a nostalgic touch, and largely unique in terms of content and narrator. Some of them deepen knowledge of already-known events; others provide completely new perspectives or add new parts to the story. Missing, however, is a more unified and coherent narrative.

## *Interview material from radio, television and press conferences*

The worldwide interview material from radio, television and press conferences in which the Beatles talk about the Hamburg period is scarce, and of the nearly 150 interviews and press conferences preserved from 1962 to 1969 in 'The Beatles Interviews Database', the most complete source on the subject, only a little more than a handful relate to the Hamburg era. If you only look at British material, the sources are even fewer.

However, two examples of interest can be cited. The first is a radio interview that the band gave to Radio Clatterbridge, a hospital radio station based at Clatterbridge Health Park, Wirral, UK, at the end of October 1962. Here the band talked about how Williams got them their first contract in Hamburg, but also about their dislike of the Hamburg recordings (Radio Clatterbridge 1962). The other is the BBC TV documentary 'Mersey Sound', which was originally broadcast on British TV on 9 October 1963, but was recorded at the end of August of that year. Here the group recounted how it was in Hamburg that they learned to 'Mach Schau' [make a show] and found their style. They also recounted how, on their return to Liverpool in December 1960, they were billed as 'Direct from Hamburg', leading the home crowd to believe they were a German band (BBC 'Mersey Sound' 1963).

## The official narratives

The 'official narratives' are publications by the Beatles camp themselves. These are also the first narratives in which the Hamburg era is retold in a more coherent form and with an agenda. The publications are fewer in number than in the other two narratives, but greater in volume and more collected in format. The narratives from the 1960s also had the greatest spread and impact.

### The Shepherd storyline of 1963/1964

The first official, more unified material on the Hamburg period can be found in the series of articles 'A Tale of Four Beatles' in the fan club magazine *Beatles Book* and the book *The True Story of the Beatles* (*Beatles Book* 1963–64; Shepherd 1964). Both were published at the turn of the year 1963/64 and were written by Peter Jones, editor of the *Record Mirror*, under the pseudonym Bill Shepherd (*Guardian* 2015). The book is the more content-rich of the two sources and, although published somewhat later, forms the basis of the article series.

In Shepherd's texts, many of the cornerstones from *Mersey Beat* are retold, albeit in more detail and with a chronologically coherent storyline. Several new parts are also added, and parts of the story are both emphasized differently and told in alternative ways. The sources in Shepherd are both the band members themselves and friends such as Sheridan, Kirchherr and Fascher (*Beatles Book* 1963–64/Shepherd 1964).

In the Shepherd material the image of Hamburg as a place of hard work and hard play is emphasized more clearly than in *Mersey Beat*. Here the foundation is also laid for the future story of the return to Liverpool from Hamburg in December 1960 and how, after a humiliating homecoming, the band rose from the ashes and became a top act on Merseyside. Shepherd also includes for the first time the story of Kirchherr and Sutcliffe's love affair, although, unlike a contemporary article in the German press, their influence on the Beatles' image and world of thought is not yet fully acknowledged (see *Bild-Zeitung* 1964: 5). Sutcliffe and Best's personas are also established for a wider audience. Both are portrayed as quiet, 'James Dean' types, beloved by the public but withdrawn in private. Neither of them belonged to the band's inner core, and both were almost destined to leave from the start in this telling of the story. Hamburg is also, in Shepherd's version, the place where the Beatles and Ringo Starr got to know each other and where he played his first gigs with the band. Further, the Hamburg recordings are described in more detail than in *Mersey Beat*, as also is the way in which requests for 'My Bonnie' in Epstein's record shop eventually led to him becoming the group's manager (*Beatles Book* 1963–64/Shepherd 1964). This story was also retold a few months later in Epstein's own autobiography, *A Cellarful of Noise* (Epstein 1964). Also of note is the different version of the fire at the Bambi Cinema told by Shepherd. It is stated here, contrary to earlier in *Mersey Beat*, that the cause of the fire was not McCartney and Best accidentally setting fire to a piece of cord but the ignition of a stove that got out of hand (*Mersey Beat* 1963c: 3; 1963e: 8; *Beatles Book* 1963–64/Shepherd 1964).

Finally, Shepherd also offers a number of more or less independent anecdotes that would accompany the Hamburg story going forward, sometimes in alternative versions: how the Beatles, after their return to Liverpool, were marketed as 'Direct from Hamburg' and were mistaken for a German band; how the band parodied Hitler and the Nazis on stage in the clubs in Hamburg; and how Lennon, during one of his pranks, got stuck in a TV antenna on the roof of the Top Ten Club. Shepherd also recounts how the Beatles, when they arrived for their first stint at the Star Club in April 1962, learned of Sutcliffe's death at Hamburg airport and how, during the same Hamburg stay, they received a telegram from Epstein about the Parlophone session. Even the later, oft-retold story of how Lennon walked around the Star Club with a toilet seat around his neck, wearing only swimming trunks, has its origins in Shepherd (*Beatles Book* 1963–64/Shepherd 1964). Harrison later claimed that this was his funniest memory from the Hamburg period (*Beatles Book* 1966b: 7–8).

## The Hines storyline of 1966

A three-part series of articles called 'Their First Visit to Hamburg' was written by Iain Hines and published in the *Beatles Book* concurrent with the Beatles' German tour and return to Hamburg in 1966 (*Beatles Book* 1966a). Hines's account is independent of *Mersey Beat*, Shepherd and Davies, and is instead based on his personal memories.

In the 1960s, as pointed out earlier, Hines on several occasions in both the British and American press described the Hamburg scene and his time there with the Beatles. In the *Beatles Book*, he returned to the subject one last time, on this occasion with his most detailed account. In the articles, Hines talked about his memories, from his first meeting with the Beatles in Hamburg in 1960 to his last one at the Star Club in 1962. He also wrote about everyday life in Hamburg and the people there, such as Rosa Hoffman, housekeeper at the Kaiserkeller/Top Ten Club, also known among the British groups as 'Mutti' [Mother]. Hines's memories of Hoffman included how she made sure that the Beatles got through the day with clean clothes and food, and how, when McCartney used to sit on the roof of her houseboat and rehearse, the dockworkers would gather to listen. Other main characters in these stories that do not appear anywhere else include Jim Hawk, the head of the British Seamen's Mission, who served the Beatles and other British bands cornflakes and milk, and Liane (surname unknown), the barmaid, whose home they went to in their spare time for meals and to listen to records (*Beatles Book* 1966a).

Notable also in the articles is a detailed account of the Beatles' deportation from Germany, a story which both Hines and Best had previously told in the American press but which now for the first time reached British audiences in full (see *16 Magazine* 1965: 9–12; *TeenSet* 1965: 44–48). Another anecdote that stands out is the story of how the Beatles, among other antics, walked around St Pauli in Hamburg wearing German Afrika Korps caps with small white swastikas (*Beatles Book* 1966a).

Finally, it can be noted that neither Hawk nor Liane tell their own stories in any context, although British musicians in Hamburg on many occasions spoke warmly of Hawk and his activities at the Seamen's Mission (e.g., *NME* 1964b: 7; *Fabulous* 1964: 8–9). Hoffman, on the other hand, was interviewed at the same time as the articles in the *Beatles Book* by the German *Bild-Zeitung*, and talked there about the Beatles' energy on stage in Hamburg and how she had McCartney's then-girlfriend, Dorothy Rhone, living on her houseboat when she and Lennon's future wife, Cynthia Twist, visited in 1961 (*Bild-Zeitung* 1966: 8). A few years later she also appeared in the British *Daily Mail* and described how the Beatles lived on her houseboat in Hamburg and her role as an extra mother to the band, especially McCartney (*Daily Mail* 1969: 9).

## *The Davies storyline of 1968*

*The Beatles: The Authorised Biography* by Hunter Davies is the only formally authorized biography of the band, although Shepherd's material has the same status in practice (Davies 1968). A large part of the narrative in Davies is in the author's own words, without clear sources being indicated. The named participants in the Hamburg part, however, include the Beatles themselves, mainly Lennon and Harrison, Kirchherr and Klaus Voormann. Best also makes an appearance, and many of the Hamburg recollections he previously shared in the American press resurface in the Davies biography (e.g., *TeenSet* 1965: 44–48; 1966: 40–42, 58–59, 61). Similarly, earlier interviews with Kirchherr in the German, American and British media are clearly related to her input in Davies' work (see *Bild-Zeitung* 1964: 5; *Rave* 1964: 19–24; *Motion Picture* 1964: 1–5).

Davies' narrative largely follows the same framework as Shepherd and *Mersey Beat*, repeating the mantra of Hamburg as a place of hard work, tough living conditions, crazy antics, wild living, and the place where the group turned from amateurs to professionals. Davies' narrative tone is darker, however, and he recounts Lennon's shoplifting, violent club fights, Preludin abuse, sexual escapades, and the group's failed robbery attempt on a British sailor. Tensions within the band are also addressed, as well as how the members regretted their harsh treatment of Sutcliffe and, to some extent, Best. The emphasis of Davies' narrative also differs from Shepherd's; for example, he gives the Hamburg recordings and the Beatles' time at the Top Ten Club less space, while their time at the Kaiserkeller gets more attention. What they have in common, however, is that neither gives the residency at the Star Club much space, something they also have in common with other sources from the 1960s (*Beatles Book* 1963–64/Shepherd 1964; Davies 1968).

Newly added parts in Davies are the descriptions of the Beatles families' reactions to their first Hamburg contract and a socio-economic account of Hamburg. Also new is the recognition of Kirchherr and Sutcliffe's influence on the Beatles' early clothes, hairstyles and mindset. Kirchherr's photographs of the band are also highly praised. In Davies, a different background to the Hamburg contract is also given compared to earlier in *Mersey Beat* (*Mersey Beat* 1963b: 9). In Davies' version, the centre of the story is moved to 21s in London instead of Hamburg, and the event gets a completely new context. Even the story of the fire at the Bambi Cinema is told differently. Gone is the explanation about the ignition in a stove as the cause. Now the explanation is, as Best told the US press a few years earlier, that an accident occurred when he and McCartney tried to make some light to clear out of their living quarters at the Bambi Cinema (*TeenSet* 1965: 44–48; Davies 1968).

As noted, Shepherd and, to some extent, *Mersey Beat* contain a number of more self-contained anecdotes that would accompany the Hamburg narrative going forward. From Davies came the story of how Lennon, challenged by Harrison, paraded in the street wearing only a pair of long underpants while reading an English newspaper (Davies 1968). This story was previously told in the American press by both Fascher and Best, but was now repeated for a British audience (*Motion Picture* 1964: 1–5; *TeenSet* 1965: 44–48).

## The original 1960s Beatles in Hamburg narratives – conclusions

The Liverpool narrative, based primarily on the *Mersey Beat* magazine, contains the first account of the Beatles' time in Hamburg, and many of the future cornerstones of the Hamburg narrative derive from it in terms of content and basic structure. What is lacking, however, is a coherent chronological narrative, and the impact of the narrative was also limited in that the audience it reached in the 1960s was mainly confined to Merseyside and north-west England.

The fact that the Liverpool narrative was in many cases documented in real time or very close to real time, that it has an insider's perspective, and that the Beatles had not yet achieved fame outside Liverpool makes the reporting authentic. The fact that the narrative focuses not only on the Beatles but also on other Merseyside groups who travelled to Hamburg also gives context to the story of the group's time there, something that is lost in later reporting where their Hamburg experiences are increasingly made unique and exclusive.

The Liverpool narrative changed form from 1961 to 1963, from stand-alone reporting on current events to finally being told in a more retrospective collective form. This was done through a series of articles in *Mersey Beat*, the first to summarize the group's career and the first to cover the Hamburg era in more detail. The series also marks, with a few exceptions, the end of the magazine's coverage of the group's time in Hamburg. Its post-1963 reporting instead focuses on the Beatles' ongoing careers in real time, and the focus of the Hamburg coverage shifts to the ongoing activities of other Liverpool groups there.

All British 1960s narratives of Hamburg, not just the Liverpool narrative, are based on the memories of relatively few people. The Beatles' own testimonies are most evident in the Liverpool narrative and in the official narratives. In the national narrative, various people around the band are the main sources, such as various club owners, music colleagues and friends. It should also be noted that the similarity between the different narratives is not primarily the result of a direct transfer of texts but rather a consequence of the same individuals repeating the same stories in several contexts. The differences in the narratives are thus more dependent on the choice of narrator than anything else.

The national narrative brings together the story of the Beatles' time in Hamburg as told in the British pop and youth press and in interview material from radio, television and press conferences. Of these, the press material is the main source. In the 1960s the pop and teen press was a central transmitter of rock and pop culture to teenagers, and its readership was large, both within and beyond Britain. The Hamburg material in these papers was, in turn, varied in content and included everything from record reviews to interviews with key figures from the Hamburg scene, and most of the stories were also unique and rich in detail. However, the pop and teen press periodical format, as with *Mersey Beat*, limited the stories' impact, and the fact that the Hamburg features, unlike in *Mersey Beat*, were scattered across many different papers makes the Hamburg stories in these sources even more of a puzzle without context. It was only later, through publications such as Mark Lewisohn's books starting with *The Beatles Live!* (Lewisohn 1986) and, for example, through publications such as Thomas Rehwagen and Thorsten Schmidt's *Mach Schau: Die Beatles in Hamburg* (Rehwagen and Schmidt 1992), Hans Olof Gottfridsson's *The Beatles: From Cavern to Star Club* (Gottfridsson 1997), Thorsten Knublauch's *The Beatles Mach Schau in Hamburg* (Knublauch 2021) and others that more coherent contexts were created from the parts.

The national narrative is largely independent of the other narratives, even if a certain connection exists through the same narrators. No clear overall trends in the material can be discerned either. The reasons for the decline in articles about Hamburg after 1965 are also not fully understood. It is possible that the stories that could be told had been told, and their news value had disappeared. The release of the Hamburg recordings in the UK, around which much of the music press's interest in the Hamburg era had revolved, had also largely ceased by this time, and the fact that the British Hamburg scene in general was also in decline from the mid-1960s onwards probably also further reduced interest.

The official narratives can be divided into three different tracks: 'the Shepherd storyline of 1963/1964', 'the Hines storyline of 1966' and 'the Davies storyline of 1968'. These represent the only Hamburg narratives from the 1960s that have a coherent chronological storyline. However, it should be noted that neither the official narratives nor any other narrative from the 1960s fully render the time, place and context of various events during the Hamburg period accurately. Only later, with publications such as Lewisohn's and others, does research into the Hamburg period become more exploratory in nature, with events placed in their proper chronological context.

As the Hamburg story was told in a coherent format, a clearer agenda followed. The different storylines were also formed at different points in the group's career. When Shepherd wrote his texts, the band were in their foundational phase, and there was little knowledge of them outside Liverpool. The basic features of the band's history had to be told to a new audience. The Hamburg period was also still a relatively large part of their overall career and was also close in time. When Davies' storyline was formed, the Beatles were both well known and well established, and the Hamburg period more clearly represented a past time in their history. In Davies' storyline the boy band image is also less prominent, and their views on, for example, drug use are more liberal, and stories about crime, sexual escapades and violence are less toned down. Similar examples of the influence of the zeitgeist on the Hamburg story, although from a completely opposite perspective, can be found in the Beatles' parodies of Hitler and the Nazis, which are told in all three storylines and which today would be more politically charged than in the 1960s.

Both Shepherd's and Davies' stories have a clear connection to the Liverpool narrative. Davies also builds on Shepherd in his narrative. Hines's Hamburg narrative, in turn, stands free from Shepherd and Davies, and is instead entirely based on his personal memories of the Beatles. Some limited connections also exist to the national narrative, which depends on the same narrator.

Most normative for the Hamburg story as a whole, not only in the 1960s but also later, are Shepherd's and Davies' storylines, mainly because the biographies in which they appeared were published in several languages and sold millions of copies. The Hines storyline, published only in the *Beatles Book*, had a much smaller impact. The same goes for the Liverpool narrative and the national narrative.

## Acknowledgements

Thanks to Melissa Davis, Thorsten Knublauch, Peter Sims and Jacques Volcouve.

## Bibliography

### Books

Davies, Hunter (1968) *The Beatles — The Authorised Biography* (London: Cox and Wyman).
Epstein, Brian (1964) *A Cellarful of Noise* (London: Souvenir Press).
Gottfridsson, Hans Olof (1997) *The Beatles: From Cavern to Star Club* (Stockholm: Premium Publishing).
Gottfridsson, Hans Olof (2001) *Beatles Bop — Hamburg Day* (Bear Family Records Hambergen). Released together with the CD box 'The Beatles with Tony Sheridan Beatles Bop — Hamburg Days' (Bear Family Records BCD 16447 BK).
Knublauch, Thorsten (2021) *The Beatles Mach Schau in Hamburg* (Doorwerth: Apcor Books).
Krüger, Ulf (2010) *Der Bekannteste Beat-Club Der Welt/The Most Famous Beat-Club in the World* (Höfen: Hannibal Verlag).
Lewisohn, Mark (1986) *The Beatles Live!* (London: Pavilion Books).
Lewisohn, Mark (2013) *The Beatles Tune In* (London: Little Brown).
Puckett, Kent (2016) *Narrative Theory: A Critical Introduction* (Cambridge: Cambridge University Press).
Rehwagen, T., and T. Schmidt (1992) *Mach Schau: Die Beatles in Hamburg* (Braunschweig: EinfallsReich).
Shepherd, Billy (1964) *The True Story of the Beatles* (London: Beat Publications).

## Newspapers/magazines

*16 Magazine* (1965) 'Beatles Secret Wild Pix. Part One: The Night the Beatles Were Kicked out of Hamburg — by Iain Hines', January.

*Beat Instrumental* (1966) 'Those Days in Hamburg — by John Emery. Parts 1–3', March–May.

*Beatles Book* (1963–64) 'A Tale of Four Beatles by Billy Shepherd. Parts 1–7', September–April.

*Beatles Book* (1964) 'Hamburg Stamp', December.

*Beatles Book* (1966a) 'Their First Visit to Hamburg by Iain Hines. Parts 1–3', July–September.

*Beatles Book* (1966b) '"I've thrown away 30 songs", says George', October.

*Bild-Zeitung* (1964) 'Eine Hamburgerin erfand die Erfolgsmasche der "Pilzköpfe"', 24 February.

*Bild-Zeitung* (1966) 'Die Beatles und Icke von Dietrich Hesse und Rolf H. Kramer', 13 June.

*Cashbox* (1964) 'Germany — Review 1964', 26 December.

*Combo* (1964) 'He Introduced the Big Beat to Germany. Tony Sheridan Seeks his Future in England', 6–19 March.

*Daily Mail* (1969) 'POP Hamburg: The Search Goes on. Frau Rosa ... Waiting for that Elusive Golden Egg', 11 November.

*Disc* (1962a) 'Disc Date', 13 January.

*Disc* (1962b) 'Beatles Find Showbiz Isn't All Fun', 24 November.

*Disc* (1964) 'Tony Sheridan Tells that Story behind that Old Disc — by Penny Valentine', 6 June.

*Disc and Music Echo* (1966) 'Scene', 13 August.

*Fabulous* (1964) 'Our Faithful Sleuth, Betty in Hamburg Did Some ... Beatle-tracking', 9 May.

*The Guardian* (2015) 'Peter Jones Obituary', 2 August, https://www.theguardian.com/media/2015/aug/02/peter-jones (accessed 24 January 2024).

*Liverpool Echo* (1961) 'Folks — And Things They Do', 10 August.

*Liverpool Echo* (1962a) 'Off the Record by the Disker', 13 January.

*Liverpool Echo* (1962b) 'Tween Grooves', 20 January.

*Liverpool Echo* (1962c) 'Probe into Mystery Death of City Student. Mother in Germany: Father Cannot be Told', 14 April.

*Liverpool Echo* (1962d) 'Tween Grooves', 26 May.

*Melody Maker* (1962a) 'Jerry Dawson's Newsbox', 6 January.

*Melody Maker* (1962b) 'Newsbox by Jerry Dawson', 4 August.

*Melody Maker* (1963a) 'Beatles Blast Own Hit Disc! 3-Years-Old Record "terrible — could be anybody"', 22 June.
*Melody Maker* (1963b) 'Ray Coleman and Chris Roberts Find Out ... What Makes the Beatles B-E-A-T', 3 August.
*Melody Maker* (1964) 'Beatles in Disc Storm — Lennon "Solo" Issued', 30 May.
*Mersey Beat* (1961a) 'Being a Short Diversion on the Dubious Origins of the Beatles. Translated from the John Lennon', 6—20 July.
*Mersey Beat* (1961b) 'Beatles Sign Recording Contract!', 20 July—3 August.
*Mersey Beat* (1961c) 'Well Now — Dig This! — by Bob Wooller [sic]', 31 August—14 September.
*Mersey Beat* (1961d) no title, 30 November—14 December.
*Mersey Beat* (1961e) 'Mersey Roundabout by Virginia', 3—17 August.
*Mersey Beat* (1961—62a) 'Prediction Notes from NEMS', 14 December—4 January.
*Mersey Beat* (1961—62b) 'The Roving "I" — by Bob Wooler', 14 December—4 January.
*Mersey Beat* (1962a) 'Mersey Roundabout by Virginia', 25 January—8 February.
*Mersey Beat* (1962b) 'Goodbye Stu!', 19 April—3 May.
*Mersey Beat* (1962c) no title, 3—17 May.
*Mersey Beat* (1962d) 'News from Germany', 3—17 May.
*Mersey Beat* (1962e) 'New Record', 12—26 July.
*Mersey Beat* (1962f) 'High Jinks in Germany', 20 September—4 October.
*Mersey Beat* (1963a) 'The Beatles Story Parts 1—11', 11—25 April to 29 August—12 September.
*Mersey Beat* (1963b) 'The Beatles Story Part 3', 9—23 May.
*Mersey Beat* (1963c) 'The Beatles Story Part 4 by Paul McCartney', 23 May—6 June.
*Mersey Beat* (1963d) 'The Silver Beatles. Howie Casey Tells of the Beatles First Trip to Hamburg. The Beatles Story Part 6', 20 June—4 July.
*Mersey Beat* (1963e) 'In His Own Words: Pete Best Tells of — My Beatle Days. The Beatles Story Part 10', 15—29 August.
*Mersey Beat* (1963f) 'Germany's Centre of Beat', 10—24 October.
*Mersey Beat* (1963—64), 'Unlucky Lu', 19 December—2 January.
*Mersey Beat* (1964) 'First Beatles Colourpic', 12—26 March.
*Motion Picture* (1964) 'The Beatle Who Died', September.
*New Record Mirror* (1962) 'We Made Sure of Applause — We Took Our Fans with Us. Reveal the Beatles', 24 November.

*New Record Mirror* (1963a) 'The Hamburg Scene by David Griffiths', 6 April.
*New Record Mirror* (1963b) 'Can that Disc Harm the Beatles? "My Bonnie" Release Was Cut 3 Years Ago!' 1 June.
*New Record Mirror* (1964) 'The New 3-Years Old Beatle Disc – by Peter Jones', 30 May.
*NME* (1962a) 'Potted Pops', 5 January.
*NME* (1962b) 'Liverpool's Beatles Wrote Their Own Hit', 26 October.
*NME* (1962c) 'Beatles LP Fixed', 30 November.
*NME* (1963) 'The New Disc Stars of 1963 Look Back on 1962 and Tell Allan Smith Christmas Was Never Like This Before. Beatles Had Fish for Xmas Dinner!', 20 December.
*NME* (1964a) 'Tony Sheridan for Liverpool', 21 February.
*NME* (1964b) 'Cordell Marks Talks with Singer Tony Sheridan about the Hard-up Days of the Beatles', 20 March.
*NME* (1964c) 'The Early Beatles', 29 May.
*NME* (1966) 'Back to the Scene of Misery & Poverty. Beatles Return to Hamburg. *NME*'s Chris Hutchins Goes with Them', 1 July.
*NME* (1968) 'George is a Rocker Again', 21 September.
*Observer* (1968) 'The Tragic Fifth Man – Nik Cohn Explores the Sutcliffe Legend', 8 September.
*Pop Weekly* (1962) advertisement, 22 December.
*Rave* (1964) 'I Filled my Beatle's Last Days with Love – by Ed Blanche', September.
*Record Mail* (1962) 'The Beatles Play Original Rock'n'Roll', 11 November.
*Record Mirror* (1964) 'The Beatles Deported – by David Griffiths', 10 October.
*Record and Show Mirror* (1960) 'Could Click with Rock on the Sousaphone', 19 November.
*The Stage and Television Today* (1962) no title, 22 November.
*TeenSet* (1965) 'Part 1: The Fifth Beatle. Pete Best's Exclusive Story', November.
*TeenSet* (1966) 'Part 2: The Fifth Beatle', February.
*Tewkesbury Register* (1962) 'Sue's Column. Stepping it out with Youth', 2 February.

## *TV and radio*

BBC, 'Mersey Sound', 9 October 1963, https://www.youtube.com/watch?v=gwTuTlH2N98 (accessed 9 January 2023).

Radio Clatterbridge, 28 October 1962, https://www.radioclatterbridge.co.uk/the-beatles-on-radio-clatterbridge (accessed 10 January 2023).

## Digital sources

The Beatles Interviews Database, http://beatlesinterviews.org (accessed 7 May 2023).

# Listen to what the man said
## McCartney and journalistic objectivity – a test case

Martin Shough
*Independent author*
*parcellular@btinternet.com*

**Abstract:** In 2009 the magazine *Prospect* published an interview with Paul McCartney in which he described a 1966 meeting with philosopher Bertrand Russell (Power 2009). McCartney recalled discussing Russell's moral objections to the war in Vietnam and later reporting these back to the other Beatles in terms that impressed them, at a time when they had yet to become vocal on the subject. Press reaction was largely derisory, couched in terms that prompted the article's author to publicly criticize a pattern of reflexive misrepresentation of McCartney in the press. Typically, journalists scorned McCartney's account, to the extent of doubting that a meeting with Bertrand Russell occurred at all. McCartney was widely accused of rewriting history to cast himself in the kind of political and intellectual role more typically accorded to John Lennon.

We attempt to clarify this dispute with reference to documentary and anecdotal sources, finding independent evidence not only that this meeting occurred but also that, upon learning that McCartney was pursuing an anti-war film vehicle for the Beatles, Bertrand Russell actively facilitated a meeting between McCartney and novelist and producer/screenwriter Len Deighton; in the same time frame McCartney was meeting with civil rights and Vietnam war crimes activist Mark Lane, then a director of Bertrand Russell's Peace Foundation, to discuss the New York attorney's controversial book on the Kennedy assassination, the film version of which McCartney subsequently offered to score. The fact that McCartney was apparently alone in pursuing projects of this sort at this time, months before film director Dick Lester announced John Lennon's acceptance of a part in *How I Won the War*, is in tension with popular narratives in which he is portrayed as a follower and superficial tunesmith. Journalistic accusations of dishonesty on the part of McCartney in

2008 are here examined and rebutted, and specific questions raised about the claimed timeline of events in 1966 are addressed in detail.

The argument is of obvious interest in Beatles historiography, as accusations of self-serving revisionism on the part of McCartney have become a commonplace of fan criticism, especially since the death of Lennon. More generally, it speaks in a timely way to wider concerns about declining journalistic professionalism and integrity (Newman and Fletcher 2017), and related issues of poor media literacy and an increasing public mistrust of traditional news and opinion sources (Gibson et al. 2022).

**Keywords:** Paul McCartney, *Prospect*, Jonathan Power, Bertrand Russell, Mark Lane, Len Deighton, Vietnam, anti-war

> McCartney won't tell you [the truth]. He rewrites history. All the time.
>
> Philip Norman, Beatles biographer (1987)

## 'A cat's cradle of self-invention'

Reflecting the commonplace that John Lennon was the intellectual Beatle, the political Beatle, newspapers around the world pilloried Paul McCartney in December 2008 in relation to an interview with the highbrow politics and current affairs monthly *Prospect* (Power 2009), convicting McCartney of outrageous self-aggrandizement. According to them, McCartney claimed that he had been the one to 'radicalize' John Lennon and to influence a whole generation after meeting with Bertrand Russell and persuading the Beatles to follow the pacifist philosopher's denunciation of what McCartney called the 'bad war' in Vietnam.

'"I politicised the Beatles" — Sir Paul McCartney claims that he persuaded John Lennon to oppose Vietnam', trumpeted the *Telegraph*, objecting with the *non sequitur* that 1960s student activist Tariq Ali didn't recall McCartney becoming prominent in the peace movement. Critics of McCartney would see this as 'a further attempt', said the paper, 'to revise the history of the Beatles, casting himself in a better light' (Leach 2008). '"I politicised the Beatles," McCartney insisted', alleged the *Guardian*, open-mouthed with disbelief, wondering if we should henceforth deconstruct 'Ob-La-Di, Ob-La-Da' as 'a commentary on American neo-colonialism' (Michaels 2008). The *Independent* even suspected a bald lie, musing that it was 'the detail about Bertrand Russell that makes one sceptical' of McCartney's 'extraordinary cat's cradle of self-invention'. A man who 'exists in a heady stratosphere of Olympian fawning', it said, rolling its eyes, would of course *have* to be 'briefed on world events only by the global A-team' (Walsh 2008). McCartney's recollection that previously 'most of us didn't know about [Vietnam], it wasn't yet in the papers' was derided (Walsh 2008). The very idea that his childish characterization of Vietnam as 'a bad war' might have owed anything to a mind as subtle as Bertrand Russell's was lampooned. McCartney was clearly on a mission to polish his image by 'revising history' (Leach 2008).

However, none of these papers reported it when the interviewer and author of the *Prospect* article, Jonathan Power, accused journalists of manufacturing a story by wilfully 'twisting the words' of McCartney. It was 'as if the press has a mind-set about the McCartney–John Lennon relationship that demands that anything he says be squeezed into some previous mould', he said, complaining that they selectively lifted phrases from his 5000-word interview (Power 2008). In fact, it was worse than that. Far from 'insisting' that 'I politicized the Beatles', nowhere in the interview does this gleefully requoted headline, or an analogue thereof, occur at all. Neither does McCartney anywhere claim to have been any kind of leading figure in the peace movement. He barely mentions John Lennon, and certainly doesn't claim that he 'radicalized' him.

McCartney had not sought a political platform, but agreed to a request for an interview from Power, whom he had known as a schoolboy at the Liverpool Institute. 'Paul is not known for his political views', Power's article began. 'John was always thought of as the political Beatle. But having been a political journalist for most of my life I wanted to talk to Paul about, among other things, the great political events of our lifetimes' (Power 2008). Power was taken aback by how deeply unwelcome the result proved to be among his fellow journalists. But McCartney was probably not so surprised by sneering caricatures such as this one by Sean Michaels in the *Guardian*:

> 'I politicised the Beatles,' McCartney insisted. And now he has passed the 'megaphone' to a new generation of political artists, he said. People like Bono. Bono, meanwhile, was honoured in Paris this weekend, at the Peace Summit. 'I am an over-awarded, over-rewarded rock star,' Bono said after receiving the Man of Peace prize. 'You are the people who do the real work.' Somewhere in England, Paul McCartney is squeaking: 'Me too!' (Michaels 2008)

Here, Michaels is wilfully misrepresenting the following exchange in McCartney's interview. Power had mentioned to McCartney a recent film (*Across the Universe*, 2007), whose director claimed that the Beatles, collectively, had 'transmitted the mood of the 1960s' in a unique way. Did Paul think this was true?

'Maybe', Paul shrugged. 'But the nice thing about it was that we didn't do it consciously. We sort of stumbled into things.' It was at this point McCartney offered the Russell meeting as an illustration.

'You [still meaning the Beatles] were a megaphone for a generation', persisted Power. To which McCartney replied, 'We thought of ourselves as just sensible young people. We didn't think we were especially wild. There were millions of people, we were part of a movement. We weren't the worst by a long shot. We were rather innocent. Perhaps in terms of responsibility we did sow some seeds for people who came after. People like Geldof, Bono, people who have the megaphone now.'

'Did you contribute to social progress?' Power pressed.

'In an innocent way, almost unintentionally', conceded McCartney, 'I think we made a contribution.'

So not only was McCartney *not* claiming to have personally 'passed the megaphone' — this metaphor was introduced by the interviewer, and in relation to the Beatles — he was not even claiming a major social role for the Beatles collectively, merely conceding a degree of truth in someone else's claim that theirs had been a significant voice in the 1960s. He does not say that he radicalized the Beatles or Lennon. What he does say is that when he described Bertrand Russell's articulate anti-Vietnam argument to the other Beatles, it was *one* of the catalysts, along with the accelerating impact of the draft on American friends of theirs, that started to make them — Lennon especially — more motivated to speak about Vietnam, and helped encourage their opposition to the war in the summer of 1966.

This is a fairly anodyne statement. One has to wonder what it is about McCartney that can turn journalists into contemptuous parodists — as in this 'sceptical' reaction from John Walsh in the *Independent*:

> So Paul McCartney not only wrote songs in the 1960s, he energised a whole generation to protest against Vietnam, because he learnt about it at the knee of Bertrand Russell, the most famous anti-war protester in England; you'd think that, in a way, a torch was being passed from one generation to the next... If we learn in the future that McCartney also invented the Pill and the sky-ray lolly, or that T S Eliot begged him, in 1962, to collaborate on Four More Quartets, I won't be surprised. (Walsh 2008)

Walsh's excitability is unnecessary. There is nothing very controversial about any of these events. They form a minor backwater of Beatles biography of which few writers appear to be much aware — journalists least of all — but dabbling in it tends to confirm McCartney's account and in fact gives it some surprising context, as we can show from independent documentary sources.

## No music for JFK

Some readers of the book *Last Word* by the late Mark Lane,[1] summarizing decades of the New York attorney's research into the Kennedy assassination, may have been surprised that among 'many friends ... who have supported my work', Lane lists, along with Lord Bertrand Russell, one Paul McCartney (Lane 2011: 113). Pulling on this thread starts to unravel a web of surprising associations.

---

1. Mark Lane died in May 2016 aged 89.

Russell had been motivated to form his 'Who Killed Kennedy?' committee of sceptical British intellectuals in 1963 based largely on the early work of Mark Lane (Russell 1998: 640, 682), and himself published articles critical of the Warren Commission Report and of what he saw as the supine gullibility of the American press. Russell championed Lane wholeheartedly, giving him support and a roof over his head in London, near Worlds End, Chelsea, in a Kings Road flat owned by his Peace Foundation, of which Lane became a director. Here Lane worked on his first Kennedy book, *Rush to Judgment* (1966), and it was here that Paul McCartney visited him in early 1967 to discuss scoring a film adaptation of that book.

But Lane had first met McCartney the previous year, at least three times: once at a London gathering which Lane described as 'a small party of about a dozen people' (Lane 2012: 162); then again a few days later on a visit to the musician's Cavendish Avenue house (where he also met John Lennon and joined the two musicians for baked beans on toast);[2] and then a third time for a one-on-one evening of discussion with McCartney about the Kennedy assassination (Lane 2012: 163—64). We don't know where the London party took place at which Lane first met McCartney.[3] The date is also unknown. But since the first meeting was before the publication of *Rush to Judgment* on 13 August 1966 (by which date the Beatles were already out of the country on the start of their US tour),

2. Note that although McCartney and his girlfriend Jane Asher didn't properly move from her family home in Wimpole Street into 7 Cavendish Avenue until the summer of 1966, McCartney had bought the house for them in April 1965 and had begun furnishing it within days (Miles 1998: 157). It became a frequent meeting place for the Beatles before or after recording sessions at nearby Abbey Road.

3. At first sight, one possibility is that it was on an occasion described by McCartney biographer Howard Sounes at which Paul and Jane Asher together visited Bertrand Russell in the philosopher's townhouse at 43 Hasker Street (Sounes 2010: 139). Asher's presence as McCartney's partner for the evening would fit a more formal party by invitation, subsequent to the impromptu solo visit described several times in print by McCartney, and Lane would be a plausible guest. But this is speculation, and there is some doubt that such a visit ever took place. Sounes has confirmed to the author (email, 16 January 2017) that his source for the story is SAGA Magazine, October 2007; however, while Asher therein recalls fearing the atom bomb and the risk of world war in the 1960s there is no mention of any visit to Bertrand Russell.

McCartney must have first met Lane no later than the end of July 1966, and, because Lane was still editing a draft of his manuscript at the time, very probably some time in the early spring.

None of the meetings with McCartney is explicitly dated by Lane, but an anomaly in his recall reveals one clue that supports an early spring date for their first encounter. As mentioned above, McCartney met Lane again in early 1967 at Lane's Kings Road flat to discuss the forthcoming documentary film version of *Rush to Judgment*, some months after the book's publication (Lane 2012: 174). McCartney had offered to write a musical score for it 'as a present'. (Asked why he would put his reputation at risk so generously, Paul explained that one day his children were going to ask him what he did with his life, and he couldn't just answer, 'I was a Beatle.') Lane says that during the visit to his flat to discuss the film McCartney played him a brand new song on his guitar, a 'haunting and sad' song about 'all the lonely people and some father darning his socks at night' (Lane 2012: 174–75), and that he thereby became the first non-Beatle to hear 'Eleanor Rigby'.[4]

However, any meeting concerning the film of *Rush to Judgment* would be about a year too late for 'Eleanor Rigby', which was being finished when Lane was still writing the book, and had been released on *Revolver* and as a single before the book was published. (The film version of *Rush to Judgment* appeared in June 1967, the same month as *Sgt. Pepper's Lonely Hearts Club Band*.) So, if Lane is correct that 'Eleanor Rigby' was brand new and unheard when Paul played it for him, his memory is evidently conflating two different occasions. An earlier opportunity to have heard the song would have been when McCartney invited him to Cavendish Avenue a few days after the party. If so, and given that the song was by this time in the somewhat mature form described by Lane, it would imply that this early meeting must have occurred at some

---

4. Lane was keen and set up a meeting with his director, Emile de Antonio, who evidently had no interest in a Beatles contribution. In spite of Lane's urging, De Antonio vetoed the idea on the grounds that a Beatles score would distract from the necessity to present the film as a 'stark and didactic' documentary (Lane 2012: 175–76).

time between late January and early March, 1966[5] — which, as we will see, puts it in the same likely timeframe as McCartney's visit to Bertrand Russell.

According to Lane, at the party the young musician introduced himself, unnecessarily, seeming 'remarkably modest ... because he was young and not impressed with his [own] accomplishments' (Lane 2012: 162). He'd heard that Lane was writing a book on the assassination and asked to borrow the still unpublished — indeed, still unfinished — manuscript. Lane appears to have been amiably bewildered by McCartney's world and the musician's interest in his work, but he obliged. McCartney sent the mimeographed MS back to Lane 'a few days later', then telephoned that same evening to say he was convinced, inviting Lane to discuss it further over dinner the next day. Lane then visited him at Cavendish Avenue. After another few days they met again for an evening at a Polish restaurant where they remained in discussion long after the door had been locked (Lane 2012: 163).

From whom had McCartney heard about Lane's work? Not from Lane himself. Of course, it might well have been mentioned by someone else at the party. But it is possible that he knew of it already from Bertrand Russell's assistant, Ralph Schoenman, who was associated not only with Mark Lane but also, it turns out, with Paul McCartney.

## 'I'd like to meet Mr Russell if possible'

McCartney has several times told the story of visiting Bertrand Russell in terms that make it seem like a random impulse — someone told him that the celebrated man lived nearby, and he decided to pitch

5. McCartney developed the first verse, chorus and a sketch of the rest, including 'Father McCartney [a placeholder-name later changed to McKenzie]', during January. From 3 to 20 March he and Jane were away, first in Germany then in Klosters, Switzerland, where he had a version finished enough to play for some guests at the Gasthaus Casana (Turner 2016: 107). Some further lyrical embellishments were made with the assistance of the other Beatles before the first recording session on 28 April.

up at the door out of sheer curiosity, trusting to his Beatle status to get him in. For example, in his *Prospect* interview McCartney said, 'I just took a taxi down there and knocked on the door. There was an American guy who was helping him, and he came to the door and I said, "I'd like to meet Mr Russell, if possible." I waited a little and then met the great man ...' (Power 2009).

Similarly, he had told Barry Miles many years earlier:

> Bertrand Russell lived in Chelsea in one of those little terrace houses, I think it was Flood Street [it was actually Hasker Street]. He had the archetypal American assistant who seemed always to be at everyone's door that you wanted to meet. I sat round waiting, then went in and had a great little talk with him. Nothing earth-shattering. He just clued me in to the fact that Vietnam was a very bad war. (Miles 1997: 125)

This narrative certainly feeds into the media caricature of naive pop-star-about-town. But there is a little more to it than this. The elderly Russell was a man with extraordinary private and public demands on his time in this period. On his brief and busy visits to London he did not usually have the luxury of entertaining random visitors; and McCartney's arrival on the philosopher's doorstep was evidently not quite as impetuous, nor quite as unexpected, as he sometimes allows us to think.

Russell complained in his autobiography about the impossible number of people 'who wish to see me about this or that' when in London, citing as an example a one-week visit in November 1966 when 'I received visits, morning, afternoon and evening, from people wishing to talk with me. But, as well over one hundred people asked to talk with me during this week, many, over a hundred, had to be refused' (Russell 1998: 662). The burden of Russell's correspondence alone was overwhelming, and most replies were drafted by secretaries or his protective assistant. So it is far from sure that even a world-famous pop star could have gained access without some intercession. That implies at least some premeditation, which in turn implies a degree of prior interest in Russell's opinions on the part of McCartney.

Given the breadth of McCartney's curiosity and eclectic experimentalism during this period, facilitated by the intellectual circle of the Asher family in whose Wimpole Street home he had been living since December 1963, and the avant-garde literary connections of friends such as Barry Miles, such an interest is not implausible. 'I'm trying to cram everything in, all the things I've missed. People are saying things and painting things and writing things and composing things that are great, and I must know what people are doing', McCartney told the *Evening Standard* in March 1966. 'I vaguely mind people knowing anything I don't know', he admitted, adding that he wouldn't want to stay young if that meant his mind had to stay young, and remarking that Bertrand Russell was a good advert for old age (Cleave 1966). This project to educate himself had led to meetings with playwrights Arnold Wesker and Harold Pinter (Peel 2002: 44), and friendships with the likes of satirical novelist William Burroughs and mathematician John Sommerville, whom he recruited to operate his experimental Montague Street 'tape lab' after a 'pleasant evening' at Barry Miles's flat during which Sommerville 'explained the principles of free-floating equations and the mechanics of producing hallucinations using flickering lights' (Miles 1997: 239). And we do have some specific evidence that Russell was one of the people whose wisdom McCartney had coveted months before meeting him.

McCartney was a hands-on supporter and bankroller of the new Indica Gallery & Bookshop opened by John Dunbar, Peter Asher and Barry Miles in 1965, a project whose impeccable avant-garde countercultural credentials would include the founding of *International Times* and the hosting of the first British exhibition by a then little-known Japanese artist called Yoko Ono. In the autumn of 1965 Paul McCartney was not only putting up shelves and designing the wrapping paper; according to Miles, he was also their 'first customer', buying books out of the stock that he and Peter Asher were storing for them in the Asher family's basement in Wimpole Street. Paul's purchases were typically 'pretty heavy', said Miles, and included 'a volume of peace studies and stuff by Bertrand Russell'.[6] Reminiscing with Miles in the 1990s, McCartney recalled

---

6. Some other titles were Ed Sanders' *Peace Eye Poems* and *Gandhi on Nonviolence*. A handwritten list of Indica volumes purchased by McCartney is in the

his reading: 'I figured [Russell] as a good speaker, I'd seen him on television, I'd read various bits and pieces and was very impressed by his dignity and the clarity of his thinking, so when I got a chance I went down and met him' (Miles 1997: 125).

This background begins to hint that McCartney's visit the following spring was not merely a frivolous celebrity indulgence, a whim of the moment; and far from just turning up to schmooze that 'American guy who came to the door', it appears that there was a degree of premeditation in it. Indeed, McCartney told Miles, 'somehow I got his number and called him up', and a telephone call to Hasker Street would no doubt have been fielded by Russell's personal assistant, the left-wing anti-war activist Ralph Schoenman, who told author Steve Turner that he and McCartney had known each other since 1964, and that he did play an unspecified part in setting up the meeting (Turner 2016: 87). In 1964 Schoenman had already been working closely with Russell for three years as his personal assistant. Not only was he the secretary of the Peace Foundation, he had run the philosopher's 'Who Killed Kennedy?' committee since 1963, and he was also the London head of Mark Lane's 'Citizens' Committee of Enquiry' into the Kennedy assassination.

In an interview with Paul Du Noyer, McCartney almost gives the game away, characterizing his approach revealingly as follows: 'Can I come round and see you? I'm interested. "Well certainly." He lived in First Street in Chelsea,[7] *I knew some American guy assisting him, and we'd talk about Vietnam* [emphasis added]' (Du Noyer 2015: 61). So, when McCartney recalls that in 1966 'someone said to me "Bertrand Russell is living not far from here in Chelsea why don't you go and see him?"' (to Jonathan Power), or 'Somehow I got his number and called him up' (to Barry Miles),

---

Barry Miles archive maintained at the British Library. See Barry Miles, interviewed in *Going Underground – Paul McCartney, The Beatles and the UK Counter-culture*, video documentary, Pride DVD, New Malden, 37:40. See also https://en.wikipedia.org/wiki/Indica_Gallery.

7. First Street is actually next door to Hasker Street where Russell lived. Talking to Miles he had recalled it as Flood Street, which is a mile away. McCartney's memory for such details is typically shaky.

or, even more elliptically, 'I knew somebody who knew somebody and I went round one day' (to Annie Nightingale [Nightingale 2011]), the suspicion arises that this 'somebody who knew somebody' might have been, if not Ralph Schoenman himself, then someone who knew both Schoenman and Russell — someone like Mark Lane, perhaps.[8] And a further inference: that in whatever way and to whatever extent Schoenman did facilitate McCartney's visit with Russell, he may have known exactly what he was doing.

In later years Russell severed his association with Schoenman in bitter circumstances. In a note ('A private memorandum concerning Ralph Schoenman') appended to his autobiography he praised Schoenman's 'optimism', 'persistence', 'determination' and 'self-assurance', qualities that he said contributed to the 'flamboyant' activist's 'prodigious driving energy' in pursuit of 'just causes', even as they also led to a tendency to count too much upon 'gestures of support and half-hearted promises of financial help' and a

> firm belief that if he but tries long and hard enough he can extract support from even the most reluctant target... On all occasions he used my reputation and any weight that my name might carry to support his own views. And he had a vastly inflated opinion of my importance. Ralph could not, of course, resist the limelight... (Clark 1976: 640—51)

What might have passed between McCartney and Schoenman, or between Schoenman and Russell, is unclear. Was the encounter encouraged by the ambitious and resourceful Schoenman with an eye to boosting the profile of the Peace Foundation? Very possibly. But it is fascinating to speculate that Russell himself might not have been entirely innocent of the potential propaganda benefits of recruiting a Beatle. At the least, it appears likely that Schoenman knew ahead of time that McCartney was coming, and may have primed his employer to receive the famous pop-cultural icon sympathetically.

---

8. It is not possible to prove it, but McCartney's first meeting(s) with Lane might have occurred before the meeting with Russell, in which case it might have been learning about Russell's and Schoenman's support for Lane that primed McCartney to seek him out.

However it came about, Russell granted McCartney half an hour of conversation. McCartney was reportedly nervous and managed to knock over a lamp (Turner 2016: 87), suggesting that he was aware enough to be intimidated by Russell's reputation. According to his own account, when he next caught up with the other Beatles in the studio he relayed Russell's analysis of the Vietnam situation, and they — Lennon especially — were also affected by it and were encouraged to take a more outspoken stance.

## Doubts about dates

Author Steve Turner thinks that 'told in this way, the story raises awkward questions' (Turner 2016: 87). Why, Turner wonders, if it is accurate, didn't the Beatles protest earlier than they did? There had been isolated prior criticisms of the war from Lennon and, most explicitly, from McCartney in January; but the Beatles apparently did not have much to say about it publicly that spring.

This, first of all, raises the question of the date of the Russell meeting. Turner offers no specific date or evidence, and actually omits the incident from his Chronology (Turner 2016: 421–31); but he apparently assumes a date in February 1966, probably on the basis that McCartney mentioned Russell on 21 March when asked by Maureen Cleave how he felt about growing old ('Bertrand Russell seems alright — I wouldn't mind being like him at all' [Cleave 1966]). This remark might mean that he had recently visited the philosopher around the beginning of March or earlier (Paul was away in Klosters, Switzerland, with Jane from 6 to 20 March [Miles 1998: 210], and his interview with Cleave was on the day after he returned to London). But that does not necessarily follow. We know that McCartney had already expressed admiration for Russell's writing and speaking from at least September 1965, long before he thought of visiting him.

A further test of the date is McCartney's memory that the meeting happened before Lennon took the part of Private Gripweed in Dick Lester's film *How I Won the War* (Miles 1997: 126). The claim can be — and, of course, is — greeted as another reason for journalistic scepticism; but, again, investigation of the Beatles' film ambitions around this time shows that the timing does fit, and also discloses by inference a little more about the context of the McCartney–Russell conversation.

In February 1966 *How I Won the War* definitely remained an idea in Lester's imagination. According to a 1999 interview (Soderbergh 1999), Lester began preparing for this 'most ambitious and foolhardy' film while still 'finishing' the musical comedy *A Funny Thing Happened on the Way to the Forum*, which had been filmed from September to November 1965. The studio 'finishing', or post-production, usually takes a good deal longer than shooting, so it would have taken several months, probably until some time in the spring of 1966 (it was finally released that October). So, if it was during this period that the first seed of *How I Won the War* was sown, then in February, with the start of shooting still six months away, the film seems certain to have been still in early pre-production. We don't know when casting decisions were made, but John Lennon's participation in *How I Won the War* was not announced by NEMS until 3 August, a month before he left to begin work in Spain. So, it is plausible that a McCartney visit to Russell in February could have predated Lester's original approach to Lennon, as claimed.[9]

It should be said that there is some evidence that would favour a date later that spring. As we will see presently, McCartney's conversation with Russell prompted the philosopher to approach author Len Deighton on McCartney's behalf with a view to facilitating a collaboration between Deighton and the Beatles on a different anti-war film project. At that time, said Deighton, he was 'deeply involved' with pre-production of the film *Oh What a Lovely War*, which became the focus of exploratory discussions with McCartney. Since Deighton did not acquire the screen rights to *Oh What a Lovely*

---

9. Were Russell and Schoenman both in London in February 1966? Russell was 94 years old in 1966 and for the last eleven years had lived most of the time at Plas Penrhyn in Penrhyndeudraeth, Wales, his trips to London being described as 'infrequent'. But it is certainly possible, although I have been unable to establish either man's whereabouts that month. An email to Ralph Schoenman from the author dated 24 January 2017 remains unanswered.

*War* until negotiations with its stage producer Joan Littlewood during a visit to her home 'in the summer of 1966' (Deighton 2014b), this might suggest a date later than February for Russell's approach to Deighton; and it is true that the likely movements of Russell and Schoenman during 1966 might fit a McCartney visit at the end of May or the beginning of June, when both men could have been at Hasker Street together around the date of the Vietnam Solidarity Campaign launch. This would still be two months before the announcement that Lennon had been offered a role in *How I Won the War*. But Deighton admits to impetuously having begun planning and writing the screenplay of *Oh What a Lovely War* before even acquiring the rights, so this is not conclusive.

What we can say is that Turner's puzzlement addresses a suggested hiatus of no more than four months, and possibly as little as one month, between the Russell meeting and the Beatles' end-of-June tour, which, thanks to John Lennon's somewhat more loquacious reaction to a Vietnam question in Tokyo, can be thought of as a preface to the furore of the upcoming American tour and a minor watershed in Beatles protest.

## Political Beatles

If we do need to explain a delay, of whatever length, between the Russell meeting and the Beatles becoming more publicly anti-war, the first thing we should consider is opportunity, or lack of it. Early spring 1966 was their 'time off' from the Beatles. They were free of tours and other major group engagements and so were not being exposed to press questioning as the Beatles. They tended to go off and do their own thing — such as visiting philosophers. John and Ringo went to Trinidad & Tobago. George, having got married in January, honeymooned in Barbados with Pattie for half of February. Paul and Jane were in Switzerland for much of March. Then in early April the Beatles came back together at Abbey Road for a fairly strenuous schedule of writing and recording prior to final mastering of *Revolver* on 22 June, followed by their flight to Munich the very next day for the start of their next tour (Miles 1998: 217).

Secondly, as McCartney told Jonathan Power in his interview, 'most of us didn't know about [Vietnam], it wasn't yet in the papers'. Cynical journalists pounced on this and took it over-literally. But let's be realistic. Of course McCartney 'knew about' Vietnam before meeting Russell: as he said himself, he and Schoenman had previously 'talk[ed] about Vietnam'. It had certainly been 'in the papers', and McCartney had himself put it there on at least one occasion: in January 1966 he had been asked by the music weekly *Melody Maker* to fill in a questionnaire. Asked what the word 'Vietnam' meant to him, McCartney's answer — 'Bombs and shooting and killing and people doing things they shouldn't' — was unusually explicit (*Melody Maker* 1966). ('I don't like what's happening there' was Lennon's elliptical answer to the same question.) Like any young people exposed to the idealistic counter-cultural mood of the time, the Beatles discussed it and weren't happy about it. In America, as early as September 1964, McCartney had spoken tentatively against the US military draft, and Lennon hinted obliquely at his disquiet in August 1965.[10]

But it 'wasn't in the papers' in the sense that awareness of Vietnam in the British media and culture lagged far behind the United States, for obvious reasons. We perhaps tend to look back through the prism of the American experience and the British and European ferment of 1968, which might give the impression that countercultural protest in the UK occurred at a higher pitch and began sooner than was really the case.

At the start of 1966, the average mainstream paper was much less curious about the Beatles' politics than was *Melody Maker*. Even as the Beatles themselves were becoming more plugged in to the issue

10. According to internet source *The Daily Beatle*, on 12 September 1964, in Boston, Massachusetts, McCartney was asked if he would 'advocate sending all young boys your age to Vietnam', responding, 'No ... [pause] Not unless they wanted to go, you know' (https://webgrafikk.com/blog/uncategorized/beatles-and-vietnam/, accessed 17 April 2024). Almost a year later, answering a press question at the start of the Shea Stadium tour about whether the Beatles would think of entertaining troops in Vietnam, John Lennon said shortly, 'I wouldn't go there, no.' He did not explain his reasons (http://www.beatlesinterviews.org/db1965.0813.beatles.html, accessed 17 April 2024).

by 1966, the press around them was also playing catch-up, both with respect to the war itself and to the novel idea that pop stars could have political opinions or be seen as countercultural bellwethers. The Beatles rarely heard Vietnam mentioned at a press conference until they went to Tokyo in June 1966, when, fielding a question about how much interest they took in the war, Lennon replied: 'Well, we think about it every day, and we don't agree with it and we think it's wrong. That's how much interest we take. That's all we can do about it ... and say that we don't like it.'[11] Yet even by this stage their disapproval of militarism was half-hearted. Only days later in the Philippines when he was asked about 'the Bomb', Lennon replied that he personally didn't lose any sleep over it, being 'preoccupied with life, not death'; and back in London after the unnerving Marcos debacle he was by no means in a pacifistic frame of mind, muttering bitterly to reporters that 'we should have taken over Manila in the war' (Turner 2016: 258). George Harrison was even less in the mood for peace and love: 'The only way I'd ever return to the Philippines would be to drop an atom bomb on it' (Miles 1998: 218).

So, by the beginning of 1966 the Beatles would already have thought of themselves as being 'against' Vietnam, reflexively, but neither for well-articulated reasons nor with any particular passion, even though for several years they had been seeing the effects of the US military call-up on the ranks of their peers and friends, who, as McCartney recalled, 'were having to go to Canada to try to dodge the draft' (Nightingale 2011). Partly this reflected the hitherto low profile of the war in the British consciousness.

America's critical news coverage mushroomed during 1965, partly because the ramping up of hostilities coincided with the unstoppable spread of TV as the nation's prime news source, household ownership having shot up from 9% to 95% during the 1950s, with over half of US viewers having colour sets by 1965 (*Encyclopedia Britannica* online, 'Television in the United States'). TV was bringing shocking and emotive images into people's homes. But UK media coverage was nothing like as intense. A majority

---

11. http://www.beatlesinterviews.org/db1966.0630.beatles.html (accessed 17 April 2024).

of the British public was still not greatly concerned about this far-off and incomprehensible war. In polls in early 1965 many had no opinion, and percentages either supporting or disapproving of American policy were mostly about even. Gallup found a small UK majority disapproving of American actions in Vietnam for the first time in April 1965, but it was not until September that the British Foreign Office noted 'increasing concern' about domestic opinion (Ellis 2014; 560). America was still widely regarded as Britain's best friend in the world.

The escalating bombing and troop build-up during 1965 was quite slow to trigger prominent protests in Britain. Although ad hoc parliamentary groups challenged American actions, British political debate had centred mostly around the government's own intentions and fears of creeping British involvement under pressure from Washington to commit troops. And Britain had its own military complications in Indonesia and Malaysia to occupy the mainstream news agenda. Most Vietnam coverage was in left-wing and communist media such as the *Daily Worker*. Early London rallies in April and May 1965 had been covered in mainstream newspapers, but while noisy, these events were still small beer on the national stage (Edmonds 1994).

However, in October and November 1965 demonstrations in London were timed to coincide with major rallies in America and were well-covered by *The Times*, *Guardian* and *Telegraph*. By the end of the year things approached a tipping point, and protest in 1966 became more vociferous. Student radicalism and the anti-war youth counterculture began to gather momentum. Even so, according to historian Anthony O. Edmonds the British anti-war movement was 'extremely fluid and difficult to pin down', exhibiting 'the usual tensions between political activism and cultural rebellion, between the raised fist and the raised joint' (Edmonds 1994). It was limited mainly to an elite of students and a university-educated middle class, was never a mass movement comparable to those in Europe and the US, and dissipated its political energy in rivalries between competing interests such as different leftist sects and CND. The reality of Vietnam was always less important in Britain, says Edmonds, than its value as a symbol, exploited for various political goals. That is why protest was slow to coalesce around a single issue until 1966, when Bertrand Russell's Vietnam Solidarity Campaign (VSC) managed to rediscover 'the "common ground" of student activism' (Fraser 1988: 112).

Against this background, and given a lack of mainstream press interest in the Beatles' political opinions, the dilatory emergence of the Beatles' public anti-war stance during a springtime of holidays and other diversions is not hard to understand. Their instinct was to approve vaguely of peace and disarmament; but before the summer of 1966 their opinions were not very focused or very well informed. 'It was disturbing for us', said McCartney recently, 'it was a mixture of all these strange things, you know, where the world was at. It was scary. But in all truthfulness, we were more in our own heads, you know, being in a band' (Howard 2016). Ringo Starr agreed: 'You know, we were lads, it was like, this is our journey, and things have been put in place, outside of our consciousness' (Howard 2016). In this they were no different from many of their British contemporaries.

It's important to remember that through this period the Beatles were also instinctively pro-American — both musically and socially. America had been their Shangri-La since their early teens. Since 1964 the adulation of American audiences had cemented their own global status and fortune. Their heroes were Elvis, Little Richard, Buddy Holly and the Everly Brothers. They disliked communism and craved wealth and success; they resented 'progressive' taxation; they valued individualism; and they were all strongly opposed to any kind of censorship of free speech (*Melody Maker* 1966). Those were broadly 'American' values. So before the summer of 1966, the Beatles' natural warmth towards America may have muted their disapproval of the war.

By August, on their American tour, they were more outspoken in abhorring the war in Vietnam, despite having been warned off the subject by their handlers. 'Whatever you do, don't talk about the war. Don't talk about the Vietnam War, it's a sore subject', McCartney remembers being told by their American publicist. 'Of course, that was the wrong thing to say to us' (Nightingale 2011).

'For years, on the Beatles' tours, Brian Epstein had stopped us from saying anything about Vietnam or the war', Lennon confirmed. 'And he wouldn't allow questions about it' (Sheff 1981: 187). But by now Vietnam had become an explosive media issue in America, and this time the questions came, and they didn't ignore them. Part of the reason is that the Beatles themselves were waking up. By the summer they were approaching their own personal tipping point, wearying of the mop-top 'puppet show', disillusioned with their role as public property after the Marcos furore in Manila. And now came the 'more popular than Jesus' hysteria in the wake of Maureen Cleave's interview.

So, several factors were conspiring to push them over the top. The cultural mood was ripe, and plausibly one of the factors in their own experience was McCartney's exposure that spring to the influence and eloquence of Britain's pre-eminent peace campaigner, Bertrand Russell; so that when they returned to America at the beginning of August they all – principally Paul and John, and especially John – answered press questions about the war rather more bluntly than an anxious management, mindful of sensitivities, had wanted them to. The interesting question is not whether the Russell factor played a part, but why the idea that it did – even the idea that it could reasonably have appeared to do so from McCartney's point of view – should trigger so much sceptical derision from journalists. And the answer appears to have more to do with personal prejudice than with historical judgement.

For far longer than the Beatles had existed, Bertrand Russell had been the thinking man's superstar, a moral and intellectual giant comparable in the popular mind with Albert Einstein; and just as it is perfectly natural for McCartney to have been impressed by the philosopher's reputation and opinions, it is unthinkable that the other Beatles would not have been impressed by his account of the meeting – of how the great man left him in no doubt that Vietnam was, as he put it in his 2009 interview for *Prospect*, 'a bad war'.

## Of bad wars and good

Ah, that phrase: 'a bad war'. Walsh in the *Independent* couldn't resist a sarcastic dig: 'A bad war, rather than one of those thoroughly decent wars of which most people approve', he scoffs (Walsh 2008), intending to paint McCartney as shallow, but instead betraying a puerile view of geopolitical conflict which might have earned him a group-hug from the sixties flower-power generation, but would at the time have bewildered mothers and fathers who had survived Hitler.

McCartney's own gloss on the phrase 'a bad war', given to Barry Miles, had some nuance: '[Russell] just clued me in to the fact that Vietnam was a very bad war, it was an imperialist war and American vested interests were really all it was about. It was a bad war and we should be against it' (Miles 1997: 125). Of course, the naive idiom is pure McCartney, the ingenuousness of a man always more likely to say 'made up a tune' than 'composed a melody' — the sort of plain talk that derails smart writers such as Walsh. But philosophers, too, appreciate the virtue of simple language, as any well-read person should know.

Much of the clarity of thought that Bertrand Russell achieved as an ethicist — and for which he had been admired by the young McCartney — is to do with investigating the practical meanings of everyday concepts, not in order to replace them with jargon but simply to understand what we really mean when we use them. Thus, Russell wrote a great deal about the concepts of 'good' and 'bad', for example in 'The Meaning of Good and Bad' in *Elements of Ethics* (1910). In 'The Ethics of War' Russell allows that justified wars may be fought 'for the good of mankind' (Russell 1915: 130), but that while certain 'wars of principle' might be 'justified', it is 'the bad part of men's principles, not the good part' that does the justifying, and that during their execution 'the bad part rather than the good rises to prominence' (Russell 1915: 136–37). Would Russell have owned the phrase 'a bad war'? Certainly. As Canadian philosopher Michael K. Potter remarks in *Bertrand Russell's Ethics*, Russell believed that 'a bad war may be justified as a "necessary evil"' (Potter 2006: 153). So it is perfectly likely that Russell himself would have used the phrase 'a bad war' in conversation with McCartney — or, come to that, with J. B. Priestley, with Lyndon Johnson, or with Albert Einstein.

'Any war that requires the suspension of reason as a necessity for support', wrote novelist Norman Mailer, 'is a bad war' (Mailer 1968). The philosopher Nietzsche believed there had never been a bad war, while Benjamin Franklin, on the other hand, thought 'there was never a good war, or a bad peace' (Franklin 1783). In 1917 Russell's book *Why Men Fight* prompted critic Horace Traubel to complain that 'writing a bad book may be as bad as fighting a bad war' (Traubel 1917: 140).

America's war in Vietnam in fact came to be held up as the exemplar of a 'bad war'. According to Mark Moyar of the US Marine Corps University, 'most academic and journalistic accounts of the war written during and shortly afterwards depicted Vietnam as a bad war that the United States should not have fought' (Moyar 2008: 37). For example, a US Naval Institute paper in the 1970s reflected: 'The widely held view is that ... we could not win because it was a bad war ... military advice is still condemned in retrospect by those who thought we were fighting a bad war' (Hughes 2016). Journalist John Pilger defied convention to assert that even the Second World War was not a 'good' but a 'bad war' (Pilger 2014), while opinions have been divided as to whether Kosovo was 'good or bad' (Chinkin 1999: 841–47); and in Afghanistan, which at first 'looked like a good war' according to *Newsweek*, 'the victory was a mirage... It's been a bad war from the start and will be to the bitter end' (Mearsheimer 2009).

## Soundtrack for a world war?

Why did McCartney seek out the famous anti-war activist Bertrand Russell in the first place, do we suppose? Not just because of his academic reputation, surely. It was largely because he was at that time the public face of opposition to Vietnam and the prominent champion of CND. Lennon might have recently claimed in Japan that he was unconcerned about that darkest terror of the 1960s, The Bomb, but the Beatles were rapidly growing up.

The threat and the imagery of nuclear disaster cast an enormous shadow over the life and the art of the era. So it is no surprise that when the Beatles needed a film vehicle, an anti-war film was considered. And, so far as we can discover, the first of the Beatles to actively pursue an option was Paul McCartney, with the aid of Bertrand Russell.

Jane Asher might not have gone with McCartney to meet Russell, but she too remembers being 'terrified' of the atom bomb and fearing another world war. 'I think', she said, 'it made us more determined to enjoy ourselves and live for the moment' (Asher 2007: 96). And it also led to McCartney telling Russell that the Beatles were interested in making an anti-war film, which is why Russell put him in touch with author Len Deighton.

Deighton was planning a film adaptation of Joan Littlewood's 1963 play *Oh What a Lovely War*, the rights to which he and Brian Duffy had recently acquired (Deighton 2013). Russell had occasion to approach Deighton for advice on his own account, and took the opportunity to recommend that Deighton meet with McCartney.[12] McCartney, who was privately interested in the techniques and styles of cinema and was himself producing homemade arty films, did meet with Deighton at his home in London's Elephant & Castle for dinner and to discuss *Oh What a Lovely War*. McCartney recalled that Deighton was 'a good cook, so that was very pleasant' (Miles 1997: 126). But as Deighton told Howard Sounes, 'Paul explained that

---

12. According to Sounes (2010: 147), 'Russell suggested Paul speak to his friend, the author Len Deighton'. But Deighton told Robert Dawson Scott that he and Russell were not friends at that time: '[Deighton] was a bit taken aback when the phone rang one day and it was Bertrand Russell. "I knew he was a famous philosopher but I didn't know he had my phone number," he says' (Scott 2006). Elsewhere, Deighton recalls that he was telephoned out of the blue by 'Russell's secretary' — Ralph Schoenman — inviting him and his wife to visit Russell's home in Wales. Russell was mainly seeking advice from Deighton about publishing contracts, but he also told him that the Beatles wanted him to write and produce an anti-war film with them, which 'came as something of a bombshell as I was deeply involved with OWALW' (Deighton 2014a).

they wanted to be in a film with more direct reference to modern war' (Sounes 2010: 139). And from Deighton's point of view, because the project was designed around music hall songs of the period, and actual First World War dialogue, there would be no place for Beatles music. Nevertheless, Deighton was 'delighted to talk with Paul McCartney and ... we enjoyed an entertaining evening. We talked into the small hours of the morning but to our mutual regret the Beatles' ideas wouldn't fit into OWALW' (Deighton 2014b). 'Sometimes I look back', said Deighton, 'and wonder what OWALW would have been like with the Beatles as the Smith family and the film directed by Gene Kelly' (Deighton reluctantly turned down Kelly as director, because he felt the director should be English).

The Beatles and Brian Epstein had certainly been pursuing options for a third film since early 1965 to meet the commitment of their United Artists contract.[13] A number of ideas were considered and eventually abandoned during the next two years. In sequence these were the western *A Talent for Loving*; the Kipling-based cartoon *The Jungle Book*; a version of Dumas' classic *The Three Musketeers*; J. R. R. Tolkien's elven epic *The Lord of the Rings*; a script called *Shades of a Personality* about a man suffering a schizophrenic disorder, which would have cast the Beatles as personae in the man's fractured mind; and finally in the summer of 1967 *Up Against It*, an adaptation of the *Shades* script by Joe Orton, involving gay sex, transvestism and a political assassination, which was considered far too risqué by all concerned (Deezen 2015).

It is a conspicuous fact that, although McCartney – acting on his own initiative – told Russell and Deighton in the spring of 1966 that he was interested in a war film as a group project, not one of the abortive Epstein-mediated film projects for the Beatles was an anti-war film. Indeed, there is no record of any other war or anti-war vehicle being considered by a Beatle, apart from Lennon's later acceptance of a minor role in Dick Lester's *How I Won The War*. It does appear that the first datable historical evidence of any active attempt, or even desire, on the part of any Beatle to get

---

13. As it turned out they would technically fulfil that obligation with 1968's *Yellow Submarine*.

behind an anti-war production is McCartney's approach to Russell, probably in February 1966, and his resultant meeting with Deighton.

## Conclusion

There is an influential, not to say dominant, critical narrative — of which the present case can be seen as an instance — according to which McCartney's attraction to people and ideas above his working-class station has to be rationalized away as a kind of self-serving affectation. For example, biographer Howard Sounes endorses Beatles ex-publicist Tony Barrow's opinion that McCartney bought his house in Cavendish Avenue, St John's Wood, 'for the purposes of self-achievement [sic], further climbing up the ladder' (Sounes 2010: 117). Sounes himself describes this as 'a further step up for Paul' in what he seems to portray as a lifelong project of social climbing, implying that by settling in central London with Jane Asher and absorbing the influence of her family's highbrow milieu, McCartney had in a canny way manoeuvred himself into just the right circumstances to secure his own advancement.

'Step one', says Sounes, 'was from Speke to a better class of council house in Forthlin Road; step two was lodging in Wimpole Street with the Ashers; step three saw him ensconcing himself among rich and distinguished neighbours...' (Sounes 2010: 117). The tone implies calculation, but there is an element here of fitting events to a narrative. Sounes's 'step one' hardly had anything to do with the little boy who was moved to Forthlin Road by his mother's change of job. Before Sounes's 'step two' came the move to London that all the Beatles made together at the behest of Brian Epstein, into the same cramped flat, because London was where their career opportunities lay. Having then fallen for Jane Asher, and also become a friend of her brother Peter, he was invited by Jane's open-minded parents to take a room at Wimpole Street, being thereby welcomed into the Asher family's intellectual life, to be sure, but, more immediately, moving in with his future fiancé — hardly a situation engineered for social advancement. And 'step three' — 'ensconcing himself among rich and distinguished neighbours' as Sounes puts it — was buying a home not just by himself but for and with Jane, and in her mind that was clearly never going to be a council flat in Streatham. It was, unsurprisingly, a nice but certainly not ostentatious townhouse within a few miles of Jane's family home, near the central London theatres and other cultural attractions that were important to her (and that were becoming so to McCartney), and also notably handy for Abbey Road studios which were almost around the corner. As Tony Barrow also put it, 'he wanted to live right above the shop' (Sounes 2010: 117).

Sounes's narrative plays into a certain media caricature of McCartney as the Beatle who was always looking out for himself, but it is silly to make a conspiracy theory out of what is easily explained as natural preference, practicality and happenstance. We should beware of confirmation bias. All of the Beatles had fancied Jane Asher, and if, instead of McCartney, it had been Lennon, Starr or Harrison who settled in modest townhouses, while McCartney had been the one to buy an immense luxury mansion in the stockbroker belt as they all did, one can easily imagine how this, too, might be portrayed as proof of his exceptionalism, materialism, self-advancement, etc.

It is beyond the scope of this article to speculate on the psychosocial origins of this critical tendency to construe McCartney's words and actions in the least flattering light. We limit ourselves to testing the particular instance of that tendency considered here, and in this case there is every reason to think that McCartney's meeting with Russell occurred as described. The exact date of his subsequent fruitless meeting with Deighton cannot be guaranteed, but his active courting of this film option is collateral evidence:

1) that the discussion with Russell at Hasker Street did indeed circle the intersection of war protest and the Beatles;
2) that McCartney was himself motivated to pursue the issue; and
3) that Russell took McCartney's interest seriously at the time.

It's only to be expected that having Russell's strong views personally relayed via McCartney would have impressed the other Beatles, and might have helped encourage them to be more opinionated about Vietnam in the summer of 1966. A collective response would not be uncharacteristic. In interviews and press conferences the word 'we' was the personal pronoun of choice. 'We're not going to vote for Ted', threatened Lennon just before the Beatles' Royal Variety Performance in 1963, making ominous eye contact with a TV camera on behalf of them all when told that Edward Heath MP did not appreciate the Beatles' diction (Brown 2020: 325). And when the Byrds' Roger McGuinn asked George Harrison if he believed in God, McGuinn was reportedly intrigued by the reply: 'Well, we don't know about that yet' (MacDonald 2008: 247). Thomas Macfarlane observes that the Beatles' expressive richness 'seemed infinitely renewable' for the reason that they 'achieved a balanced collective entity from which individual personalities could emerge as points of focus ... before receding back into the collective group identity' (Macfarlane 2016). Similarly, Ian MacDonald notes the way that many people's experience of the Beatles in person was as a near-telepathic *Gestalt*, and describes how the Beatles 'advanced through their twenties as a sort of sensory phalanx, picking up facts and impressions and pooling them between each other' (MacDonald 2008: 247). As McCartney himself said, 'The four of us were unusual. We were an entity. Mick [Jagger] used to call us the four-headed monster' (Nightingale 2011).

Of course, though the meeting with Russell did have a material effect on the general tenor of the Beatles' public attitude to Vietnam, it was far from the only factor in why they had more to say in August 1966. They themselves were changing; also, the media provocations and opportunities were very different when they were in America. But there is simply no justification for the derision hurled at McCartney in the newspapers in 2008–09. In truth none of the Beatles were very vehement at any time, or very loquacious; and the changes discernible over time are not dramatic. Despite tracks such as 'Revolution', Lennon's more vocal opposition and media activism did not really begin until the Beatles were breaking up. Yet if there can be said to be a moment, a watershed, when the Beatles took stock of their growing up, and began to turn their faces outwards towards the world, then it was the spring of 1966.

It is a fact that McCartney proactively pursued an anti-war Beatles project, apparently alone, at this time. It appears to be true that after meeting Bertrand Russell McCartney 'reported back to John ... and he then did *How I Won the War*' (Miles 1997: 126). There is no reason to assume direct causation, nor does McCartney claim it. We know that by 1966 both he and Lennon were already receptive to an anti-war message. Nevertheless, Lennon's acceptance of Lester's offer was certainly announced several months later, and the dates suggest that McCartney's meeting with Russell may very well have predated the offer itself. It is also a fact that the Beatles' anti-war press statements did increase that summer, and inferably their conversations about the issue in private followed a similar curve.

The idea that the Russell meeting was significant in the mix of events that created a watershed that spring seems natural. If there was in McCartney's mind at the time at least the appearance of a connection between these facts, then it would be perfectly understandable.

## Bibliography

Asher, Jane (2007) *SAGA Magazine*, October 2007, 96.

Brown, Craig (2020) *One, Two, Three, Four: The Beatles in Time* (Fourth Estate).

Chinkin, Christine M. (1999) 'Kosovo: a "good" or "bad" war?" *The American Journal of International Law* 93(4): 841–847.

Clark, Ronald W. (1976) *The Life of Bertrand Russell* (New York: Alfred A. Knopf).

Cleave, Maureen (1966) 'How a Beatle Lives, No 4: Paul McCartney,' *Evening Standard*, Friday 25 March 1966.

Deezen, E. (2015) 'The many unrealized Beatles film projects', http://www.todayifoundout.com/index.php/2015/12/the-many-unrealized-beatles-film-projects/ (accessed 17 April 2024).

Deighton, Len (2013) http://deightondossier.blogspot.co.uk/2013/12/recalling-great-war-len-deighton-at.html (accessed 17 April 2024).

Deighton, Len (2014a) 'Producing *Oh! What a Lovely War* – how it happened', https://www.deightondossier.net/films/ (accessed 17 April 2024).

Deighton, Len (2014b) 'The truth about the making of *Oh! What a Lovely War*', https://www.deightondossier.net/films/ (accessed 17 April 2024).

Du Noyer, Paul (2015) *Conversations With McCartney* (London: Hodder and Stoughton).

Edmonds, Anthony O. (1994) 'The Viet Nam War and the British student left: a study in political symbolism', in *Nobody Gets Off the Bus: The Viet Nam Generation Big Book*, vol. 5, no. 1–4, March 1994, http://www2.iath.virginia.edu/sixties/HTML_docs/Texts/Scholarly/Edmonds_Brit_Left.html (accessed 17 April 2024).

Ellis, Sylvia A. (2014) 'Promoting solidarity at home and abroad: the goals and tactics of the anti-Vietnam War movement in Britain,' *European Review of History* 21(4): 557–576.

Franklin, Benjamin (1783) *Letter to Sir Joseph Banks*, July 27, 1783.

Fraser, Ronald (1988) *1968: A Student Generation in Revolt* (London: Chatto and Windus).

Gibson, Hamish, Lexie Kirkconnell-Kawana and Ed Procter (2022) *Impress News Literacy Report: Lessons in building public confidence and trust*, University of Leeds/University of Derby/Economic & Social Research Council, November 2022.

Howard, Ron (dir.) (2016) *Eight Days A Week: The Touring Years*.

Hughes, Wayne (2016) 'Vietnam: winnable war?', *US Naval Institute Proceedings* (July 1977): 60–65, repr. in Thomas Cutler (ed.), *The U.S. Naval Institute on Vietnam: A Retrospective* (Naval Institute Press).

Lane, Mark (1966), *Rush to Judgment* (New York: Holt, Rinehart and Winston).

Lane, Mark (2011) *Last Word: My Indictment of the CIA in the Murder of JFK* (New York: Skyhorse Publishing).

Lane, Mark (2012) *Citizen Lane: Defending our Rights in the Courts, the Capitol, and the Streets* (Chicago: Laurence Hill Books).

Leach, Ben (2008) 'Sir Paul McCartney: "I politicised the Beatles"', *Daily Telegraph*, 14 December, http://www.telegraph.co.uk/news/celebritynews/3743977/Sir-Paul-McCartney-I-politicised-the-Beatles.html (accessed 17 April 2024).

MacDonald, Ian (2008) *Revolution in the Head – The Beatles' Records and the Sixties*, 3rd revised edition (London: Vintage Books).

MacFarlane, Thomas (2016) 'A Mosaic Approach to Abbey Road,' *Volume! Special Beatles studies* 12(2), https://journals.openedition.org/volume/4866?lang=en.

Mailer, Norman (1968) *The Armies of the Night* (New American Library).
Mearsheimer, John J. (2009) 'How Afghanistan went from good war to bad', *Newsweek*, 5 December, http://europe.newsweek.com/how-afghanistan-went-good-war-bad-75619?rm=eu (accessed 17 April 2024).
*Melody Maker* (1966) 'Pop Think-In' questionnaire, *Melody Maker*, 22 January 1966, http://alansalbumarchives.blogspot.co.uk/2013/03/nmemelody-maker-questionairres-filled.html (accessed 17 April 2024).
Michaels, Sean (2008) 'Sir Paul McCartney: I politicised the Beatles', *The Guardian*, 15 December, https://www.theguardian.com/music/2008/dec/15/paulmccartney-thebeatles (accessed 17 April 2024).
Miles, Barry (1997) *Many Years From Now* (London: Secker and Warburg).
Miles, Barry (1998) *The Beatles: A Diary* (London: Omnibus Books).
Moyar, Mark and Kim T. Adamson (2008) 'Historians at War', *Academic Questions* 21: 37–51, https://www.nas.org/academic-questions/21/1/vietnam_historians_at_war/pdf.
Newman, N. and Richard Fletcher (2017) *Bias, Bullshit and Lies; Audience Perspectives on Low Trust in the Media* (Oxford: Reuters Institute/University of Oxford).
Nightingale, Annie (2011) BBC radio interview, 3 June, http://www.radiotimes.com/news/2011-06-03/interview-annie-nightingale-talks-to-sir-paul-mccartney (accessed 17 April 2024).
Norman, Philip (1987) TV interview with Selina Scott, in 'George Harrison', *West 57th St*, CBS, https://www.youtube.com/watch?v=zFhJeCY5R3w (accessed 17 April 2024).
Peel, Ian (2002) *The Unknown Paul McCartney: McCartney and the Avant-Garde* (Reynolds & Hearn).
Pilger, John (2014) '"Good" and "bad" war – and the struggle of memory against forgetting', *The New Statesman*, 12 February, https://www.newstatesman.com/uncategorized/2014/02/good-korea-bad-korea.
Potter, Michael K. (2006) *Bertrand Russell's Ethics* (London: A&C Black).
Power, Jonathan (2008) 'Twisting the words of Paul McCartney', 23 December, http://www.oldsite.transnational.org/Columns_Power/2008/50.TwistingMcCartney.html (accessed 17 April 2024).
Power, Jonathan (2009) 'A political Paul', *Prospect Magazine*, January, http://www.prospectmagazine.co.uk/magazine/apoliticalpaul (accessed 17 April 2024).
Russell, Bertrand (1915) 'The ethics of war', *International Journal of Ethics* 25(2): 127–142.

Russell, Bertrand (1998 [1969]) *Autobiography* (London: Routledge).
Scott, Robert Dawson (2006) 'Len Deighton: The spy and I', *The Independent*, 4 January, http://www.independent.co.uk/arts-entertainment/books/features/len-deighton-the-spy-and-i-521520.html (accessed 17 April 2024).
Sheff, David, and D. Barry Golson, ed. (1981) *All We Are Saying, the last major interview with John Lennon and Yoko Ono* (New York: St Martin's Griffin).
Soderbergh, Steven (1999) 'Interviews at the BFI: Richard Lester — Part 3', *The Guardian*, 8 November, https://www.theguardian.com/film/1999/nov/08/guardianinterviewsatbfisouthbank2 (accessed 17 April 2024).
Sounes, Howard (2010) *FAB, An Intimate Life of Paul McCartney* (London: HarperCollins).
Traubel, Horace (1917) 'Why men write', *The Conservator*, 28(November): 140.
Turner, Steve (2016) *Beatles '66: The Revolutionary Year* (New York: Ecco).
Walsh, John (2008) 'No wonder Sir Paul feels he can hector the Dalai Lama for eating meat...', *The Independent*, 16 December, http://www.independent.co.uk/voices/columnists/john-walsh/john-walsh-no-wonder-sir-paul-feels-he-can-hector-the-dalai-lama-for-eating-meat-1104832.html (accessed 17 April 2024).

# 'When Paul got an idea or an arrangement in his head…'

## Inspiration, imagination, experimentation and transitions in 'Maxwell's Silver Hammer'

David Thurmaier
*University of Missouri–Kansas City, Conservatory, 5227 Holmes Street, Kansas City, MO 64110, USA*
*thurmaierd@umkc.edu*

**Abstract:** For a song that is so mercilessly maligned, Paul McCartney's 'Maxwell's Silver Hammer' contains attractive musical features that demonstrate his effortless flow of ideas. The rehearsals captured on tape reveal genuine compositional collaboration and experimentation between the Beatles that belies the harsh criticism of McCartney in particular. Cast as an absurd story about an assassin with a silver hammer, the song displays some of McCartney's best attributes such as total command of pop musical language, whimsy, avant-garde inspiration and memorable melodies. In addition, this article examines documented and potential sources of inspiration for the song, which can be viewed more richly in context as a type of murder ballad. Analysis of extant rehearsal recordings focuses attention on McCartney's search for the most effective transition between the verse and chorus of the song, reinforcing his attention to detail through experimentation in the studio. The article closes by suggesting that McCartney's musical imagination was so fertile during this period that it was inevitable that his often uninterested and uninspired bandmates would clash over the numerous sessions devoted to this song.

**Keywords:** *Abbey Road*, the Beatles, Paul McCartney, Surrealism, music theory and analysis, *Get Back* sessions

For a song that is so mercilessly maligned — described by John Lennon as 'just more of Paul's granny music' (Emerick and Massey 2006: 280–81), by George Harrison as 'fruity' (*Crawdaddy Magazine* 1977), by Ringo Starr as 'the worst track we ever had to record; it went on for fucking weeks' (Skaggs 2018), by music theorist Walter Everett as 'Rococo craftsmanship on a Gothic but hollow shell' (Everett 1999: 253), by critic John Bergstrom as 'the single Beatles song out of nearly 200 that is basically unlistenable' (Bergstrom 2009) and by author Ian MacDonald as 'sniggering nonsense' and the 'single recording [that] shows why the Beatles broke up' (MacDonald 2005: 357) — Paul McCartney's 'Maxwell's Silver Hammer' contains attractive musical features that demonstrate an effortless flow of ideas from its composer. Moreover, the rehearsals of 'Maxwell's Silver Hammer' captured on tape reveal genuine compositional collaboration and experimentation between the Beatles that belies the harsh criticism of McCartney in particular. Tracing the song's path from its nascence in India, to its extensive rehearsal during the *Get Back* sessions, to its completion in the summer of 1969 for *Abbey Road* illuminates McCartney's compositional thinking, rehearsal style and treatment of his 'music hall' songs, with 'Maxwell's Silver Hammer' the latest in a sequence following 'When I'm 64', 'Your Mother Should Know' and 'Honey Pie' (see Thurmaier 2023).

This article details and examines the imaginative — and often contradictory — source elements underlying the style, inspiration and setting of 'Maxwell's Silver Hammer'. Cast as a story about an assassin with a silver hammer, with myriad sophisticated musical touches, the song displays some of McCartney's best attributes such as total command of pop musical language, whimsy and memorable melodies. Moreover, the surrealist nature of the song's subject matter and unusual inspiration continues a longstanding trend of McCartney's interest in the avant-garde. Musically, analysis of extant recordings focuses attention on his search for the most effective transition between the verse and chorus of the song, reinforcing McCartney's attention to detail through experimentation in the studio. I draw on rehearsals from 3 and 7 January 1969 from the so-called 'Nagra' tapes, on 9 July 1969, the first day of 'Maxwell's' *Abbey Road* rehearsal, and its final production on *Abbey Road*.

Earlier scholarship on this song points out some of these segments, but the full 'Nagra' tapes discovered after their publication in 2003 contain even more useful information regarding the song's development.[1] In these examples, we hear McCartney trying to find musical solutions to vexing formal problems, and we can assess his firm, albeit playful at times, method of crafting this song so reviled by his bandmates and critics. I close by suggesting that these rehearsals show how McCartney's musical imagination was so fertile during this period that it was probably inevitable that his often uninterested and uninspired bandmates would clash over the numerous sessions devoted to this song. Even so, we also hear some fun and lighthearted moments that challenge the overwhelmingly negative reception that 'Maxwell' has received in the Beatles story.

## A poor reputation and an absurd story

The poor reputation of 'Maxwell's Silver Hammer' stems from at least two clear issues. First, as alluded to in the comments from McCartney's bandmates earlier, the song was rehearsed often, and incessantly on some days, frustrating the other Beatles. It should be noted that this was only true for the *Get Back* sessions in early 1969, as the final recording for *Abbey Road* came together efficiently over several days that summer (9, 10, 11 June, with Moog overdubs on 6 August). Second, its placement on the *Abbey Road* album sets it up for either lightweight or forgotten status. Coming after Harrison's outstanding 'Something', and before McCartney's tour de force vocal performance on 'Oh! Darling', it is not surprising that 'Maxwell' might sound like a silly trifle in context. But is the song inherently flawed due to its subject matter, is it lacking in musical quality as a *song*, or has its post-*Abbey Road* reputation been due to the aforementioned factors?

---

[1]. Notable pre-2003 sources include Everett (1999) and Sulpy and Schweighart (1997).

It is fair to say that despite the elaborate musical touches and arrangement, much of the song's notoriety comes from its absurdly violent lyrics and imagery. McCartney began writing the song in Rishikesh, India, during the Beatles' visit in the spring of 1968 – the first lines up to 'Let me take you out to the pictures, Joan' appear in a notebook called 'Spring Songs Rishikesh 1968' – but then it sat idle until the *Get Back* sessions in January 1969 (Howlett 2019: 30). The plot in short: the song's titular character, Maxwell Edison, is a violent figure who stalks people and then fatally hits them over the head with a silver hammer. Those who meet their demise include a student named Joan, Maxwell's schoolteacher, and finally a judge, who upon pronouncing the sentence for Maxwell's crimes, gets killed by the silver hammer himself. Where did such a violent story originate?

The story, and even the music to some extent, features surrealist influences, a giveaway from the inclusion of the word 'pataphysical' in the first verse (rhyming with 'quizzical').[2] 'Pataphysics refers to a concept or quasi-science that 'represents a supplement to metaphysics, accenting it, then replacing it, in order to create a philosophic alternative to rationalism' (Bök 2002: 3; see also Corbyn 2005). The 'science' displays a whimsical side, asking questions that may sound absurd; for example, even though day always turns into night, what if one day it did not? Highlighting the ridiculousness inherent in the subject, McCartney recently offered a snarkier opinion, suggesting that 'Pataphysics may have been designed to mock 'toffee-nosed academics' (McCartney and Muldoon 2021: 463).

The concept of 'Pataphysics originated in writings by the French avant-garde author Alfred Jarry, whose play *Ubu Cocu* McCartney heard on the radio on 10 January 1966 (Miles 1997: 230–31). *Ubu Cocu* is a short play, the last of a trilogy about King Ubu, a boorish figure who represents the worst sides of humanity in his callousness and greed. In the first act, a professor named Achras has a conversation with King Ubu about 'Pataphysics, and then Ubu abruptly states that his family is going to move in to Achras's house. This is followed by a visit from 'Conscience', who tries to reason with

---

2. An apostrophe precedes the word 'Pataphysics.

Ubu, but to no avail. After a 'song' from the 'Palcontents' on behalf of Ubu telling Achras to give up everything and leave Ubu alone, the professor is impaled. The play ends with Achras (suddenly no longer impaled) getting revenge on Ubu by dropping him through a trapdoor, followed by more craziness featuring discussions between Ubu and Conscience about various digestive functions, before the Palcontents make fun of bourgeois leaders.

These themes and the language used, replete with nonsense words and amusing rhymes, more closely resemble John Lennon's writing style, but clearly McCartney was enamoured by the absurdity and wordplay. Given that McCartney talked about hearing this play in interviews for many years afterwards, it seems to have impacted his songwriting that depicts more fanciful images or ideas. As such, one could even interpret 'Maxwell's Silver Hammer' in light of *Ubu Cocu*, where Maxwell resembles King Ubu (operating with disregard of morals and the law) and Achras his victims, but with the twist that Maxwell gets away with his deeds, killing the judge who was set to decide his fate.[3] This influence would comport with McCartney's other avant-garde interests at the time (for example, the experimental German composer Karlheinz Stockhausen had just appeared on the cover of *Sgt. Pepper's Lonely Hearts Club Band* at McCartney's request), and thus it is not surprising that he would find Jarry's surrealistic musings ripe for use in a song. What might be intriguing (or serendipitous?) is that McCartney remembered the word 'pataphysical' during his time in India while starting the song, and then kept it in the fully realized version, now about a serial killer.

Later, McCartney would come up with multiple explanations regarding the source of the song and its true meaning. In *Lyrics*, he recalls that stories about the 'Moors Murders', which involved five children being sexually assaulted and killed near Manchester by a pair of disturbed lovers between 1963 and 1965, were in the news and 'quite likely in my mind' (McCartney and Muldoon 2021: 463). Moreover, McCartney also states that 'Maxwell is possibly a descendant of James Clerk Maxwell, who was a pioneer of

---

3. Ken Womack (2019: 119) suggests a similar interpretation.

electromagnetism. Edison is obviously related to Thomas Edison. They're two inventor types. Part of the fun here is that Edison is connected to the lightbulb and the phonograph, and here we were making a gramophone record' (McCartney and Muldoon 2021: 463). In *Lyrics* and in earlier publications, McCartney would state that the song's lyrics could also be interpreted as a metaphor for the disintegrating business situation among the Beatles: '[the song was] my analogy for when something goes wrong out of the blue, as it so often does, as I was beginning to find out at that time in my life. I wanted something symbolic of that, so to me it was some fictitious character called Maxwell with a silver hammer. I don't know why it was silver, it just sounded better than Maxwell's hammer' (Miles 1997: 554). And one final interpretation came from John Lennon through Apple employee Tony King: 'the minute you do something that's not right, Maxwell's silver hammer will come down on your head' (Womack 2019: 119).

McCartney's and Lennon's explanations would also be in keeping with a long history of dark humour found in British comedy films, particular those produced by Ealing Studios from 1949 to 1955, popular when they were growing up.[4] One example that shares parallels with 'Maxwell' is *Kind Hearts and Coronets* (1949), starring Dennis Price and Alec Guinness. The film relates Price's attempts to redeem his family's honour and become a duke by killing the eight people ahead of him in succession through various methods. Although Price (named Louis in the film) does not use a silver hammer as his implement of choice, his victims perish through boating and hunting 'accidents', poisoning and a bomb explosion. As in 'Maxwell', the victims are unsuspecting of their fate, and despite his actions, Louis is presented as a normal person. The main difference is that Maxwell Edison seemingly gets away with his crimes, whereas the film suggests that Louis may eventually face justice based on the memoir he wrote detailing the killings.

4. I would like to thank one of the anonymous reviewers for suggesting this connection. For a thorough look at the Ealing comedy films, see Burr (1998).

## Surreal musical elements

In addition to the aforementioned elements inspiring the lyrics and story, a surrealistic influence manifests itself musically in two ways: first, the seemingly incongruous presentation of the song's violent subject matter as a kind of nursery rhyme accompanied by a singalong tune; and second, the use of the Moog synthesizer and its sound effects, which McCartney experimented with after inventor Robert Moog visited EMI studios during the recording sessions.

To illustrate the former, the verse is set in symmetrical, 'square' phrases of four measures each, with a limited vocal tessitura of less than an octave ($D^4$–$C$ sharp$^5$). The melody lies within a compact range and features decorative descending chromatic neighbour tones that hark back to gestures used in pre-rock popular song. Such examples can be heard in the lyrics 'studied pataphysical' and 'majoring in (medicine)', where the melody moves back and forth between two notes in a playful manner. As we will see, throughout the sessions McCartney strove to keep the music light and bouncy, trying out several popular song clichés that accentuate the stark contrast between the topic and its musical setting.

Fusing violent lyrics about a quasi-serial killer to a jolly, singable tune was not unique to 'Maxwell's Silver Hammer'. In fact, many similar murder ballads – story songs that include some sort of murder, often of familial or romantic relations – are set as folk songs with repeated melodic verses and simple harmonies. A comparison might be made with 'Mack the Knife', a murder ballad from *The Threepenny Opera* by Kurt Weill and Bertolt Brecht.[5] Like Maxwell, 'Mack' (Macheath) is described as a jovial, crafty man who does his dirty work on the sly ('sneaking around'), with a knife (as opposed to a hammer). Moreover, the song lists Mack's victims such as Louie Miller, Jenny Diver and Sukey Tawdry in each verse, similar to the procession of Maxwell's victims. In keeping with a common convention of murder ballad style, McCartney also sings

---

5. Jonathan Gould also notes this comparison, although he does not elaborate on the connections other than noting that John Lennon 'actually sang a few bars of "Mack the Knife" at Twickenham Studios' (Gould 2007: 577).

the song as a narrator *about* Maxwell, instead of *being* Maxwell. 'Mack the Knife' could have served as an identifiable model for 'Maxwell's Silver Hammer', since it was a famous, chart-topping hit for Bobby Darin in 1954 and a popular jazz standard recorded by the likes of Louis Armstrong and Ella Fitzgerald.

Other murder ballads by popular singers the Beatles knew might have also inspired 'Maxwell'. Lonnie Donegan, known as the 'King of Skiffle', recorded several murder ballads. His version of 'Tom Dooley' appeared on his first album in 1956 (before the ubiquitous number 1 hit by the Kingston Trio in 1958) and tells the tale of a soldier convicted of killing his unfaithful girlfriend, who was later hanged for his crime. Bob Dylan also included notable murder ballads on his early albums, including 'The Lonesome Death of Hattie Carroll', 'The Death of Emmett Till' and 'The Ballad of Hollis Brown'. Although these examples lack the absurdist humour of 'Maxwell', most of them feature singable melodies and an emphasis on the gruesome events presented in a straightforward manner, just as McCartney describes the killing spree of Maxwell Edison.

One additional intriguing possibility — perhaps subconscious — for the inspiration and structure of 'Maxwell' comes from the many crime stories that inspired British murder ballads. In particular, there was an incident in 1849 called 'The Leveson Street Murder' that took place in Liverpool and was chronicled in the *Liverpool Journal*.[6] A captain going off to sea left his pregnant wife, two boys and servant in their Liverpool home, and to assist with finances they took in a lodger, a manual labourer named John Gleeson. Gleeson concocted a plan whereby he would stay in the house and not go to work, instead hassling the servant with questions. In the end, Gleeson beat the servant and one of the boys with fireplace tongs or a shovel, stabbed the other boy with a knife, and beat the pregnant wife with a poker, after which he robbed the house and fled. All the family members eventually died, and Gleeson was hanged in a very public and spectacular manner, with an estimated 100,000 people viewing the event. The implements used in this

6. The story of the Leveson Street Murder can be found at http://www.old-merseytimes.co.uk/levesonstmurder.html (accessed 18 April 2024).

real-life murder besides a knife — tongs, a shovel and/or a poker — are analogous to a hammer in their ability to knock someone out. The sheer scale and violence of this incident must have been fixed in Liverpool's memory, and perhaps McCartney turned Maxwell into a more surreal character to mask the deeds done by a real murderer such as Gleeson.

Ballad lyrics were written about this incident, and one verse even resembles 'Maxwell' in its element of surprise:

> One day he struck the boy a blow,
> The servant's head bewilderin',
> She said her mistress won't allow,
> Such men to beat her children,
> With that the ruffian was enraged,
> With poker smashed her pate,
> He struck her while she was engaged,
> In cleaning out the grate.[7]

Making these potential connections between 'Maxwell' and murder ballads, both historical and contemporary, provides a framework for McCartney's lyrical inspiration and puts it into the context of a particular genre. Then, observing how McCartney transforms Maxwell into a surreal character illustrates his propensity for taking real-life events and giving them a slightly distorted aura. The final step of this process is to fuse disturbing events with memorable and singable music that illuminates the irony found in the dichotomy.

The inclusion of the Moog synthesizer featured throughout the song represents a second surreal musical touch, discussed later in more detail. Its use on several songs on *Abbey Road* (for example, 'Because' and 'Here Comes the Sun') adds new sound layers to each. This novel instrument, capable of playing a variety of electronic sounds, enhances the absurdity of the story in the way it is played and highlighted, especially in the second verse. As engineer Alan Parsons remembered, McCartney enjoyed finding

---

7. The lyrics to the murder ballad are at http://www.planetslade.com/broadsides/the-liverpool-lodger.pdf (accessed 18 April 2024).

new and unusual sounds to augment the song's framework: 'Paul used the Moog for the solo in "Maxwell's Silver Hammer" but the notes were not from the keyboard. He did that with a continuous ribbon-slide thing, just moving his finger up and down on an endless ribbon' (Womack 2019: 167–68). This effect ends up sounding like a theremin, an electronic instrument often used in horror or science fiction movies from the 1940s–50s (for example, *The Day the Earth Stood Still*) to suggest a ghostly or spooky atmosphere. In case of 'Maxwell', when the Moog is added to the otherwise bouncy song, it adds a new character to the mix befitting the subject matter.

Despite its attractive and intriguing features, we have seen that the other Beatles eventually found the song disagreeable and derivative; they had been through this exercise several times before. This was the latest instalment in McCartney's pre-rock era pastiche songs following 'Honey Pie' on *The Beatles*, but earlier songs in this style did not engender the same post-recording vitriol as 'Maxwell's Silver Hammer'. An important distinction, as the tapes show, is that the other Beatles were not outwardly hostile to or dismissive of the song in the studio. In *Lyrics*, McCartney claims that although 'the rest of the guys were getting pissed with me [for taking too long to record 'Maxwell's Silver Hammer']', the 'recording sessions were always good ... and there was always a great joy in working together in the studio' (McCartney and Muldoon 2021: 463). As the tapes demonstrate, McCartney's recollections were largely confirmed by the Beatles' willingness to experiment and follow just about every one of his musical and lyrical whims during the recording sessions — even if they were annoyed.

## Formal overview

'Maxwell's Silver Hammer' consists of a verse–(pre-chorus)–chorus form, flanked by interludes and instrumental solos that utilize other parts of the song. There are three verses, each one featuring different musical arrangements (addition or deletion of instruments, vocals, etc.). Harmonically, the song features several striking applied dominant chords punctuated by a prominently mixed bass part, played by George Harrison, that emphasizes the chord tones. Other notable musical touches include the aforementioned countermelodies played on the Moog synthesizer during the second verse and programmed to sound brassy during the interludes. An organ played by George Martin contributes another 'ghostly' sound during the third verse, and the song also features the persistent double-struck anvil linked to the 'bang bang' onomatopoeia at the beginning of each chorus. Although most of the song came together quickly, with McCartney coming to EMI studios having a considerable amount of the first two verses and the chorus intact from early rehearsals, the transitions or interludes between the chorus and verses underwent a process of trial and error that uncovers the Beatles' working methods late in their career. Moreover, evidence from the *Get Back* sessions indicates that all the Beatles exerted effort and offered suggestions as McCartney searched for the best way to connect the verse and chorus. Although the other three Beatles make fun of the song and joke around at times, their spirit is collaborative.

Despite this overall positive atmosphere, some scholars have identified the collaborative search for the perfect interlude on this song as further evidence of the exorbitant effort McCartney put into a song that was never slated as a single or hit. Tim Riley asserts that '"Maxwell" tries to justify itself with textural games – no two verses or refrains don the same instrumental patterns – and the linkages between sections are fussed over in a way that steals attention from what they're supposed to ornament' (Riley 1988: 317). This might be accurate, but it is also proof of McCartney's seemingly endless creativity during the sessions.

## 'Maxwell's' interludes in the *Get Back* sessions

The Beatles spent hours rehearsing the song during the *Get Back* sessions, most notably and productively on 3 and 7 January 1969. All four Beatles were present for most of the recordings, as we can hear musically and aurally. The interlude (space) between the verse and chorus runs for four bars, and it was filled by at least six different musical solutions, discussed consecutively in the following pages:

1) Repeated descending stepwise bass line: D, C sharp, B, A
2) 'Dead music': chord progression of A, Dm/A, A7, and back; neighbouring progression over an A pedal
3) Change of metre and feel into a waltz (triple metre); repeated tonic and dominant (A/D) pitches
4) One chord: an A-augmented triad with McCartney vocalizing over it
5) A fusion of no. 1 with whistling (sometimes embellished as D, C sharp, B, A or D, C sharp, B, D, A)
6) Final version from *Abbey Road*: D, F sharp7/C sharp, Bm, D/A, G, D (I, V$^{4/3}$ of vi, vi, Passing$^{6/4}$, IV, I); return of the descending bass line

The Beatles recorded the first attempt at an interlude on 3 January, the second day of the *Get Back* sessions and towards the beginning of the 'Maxwell' rehearsals (Audio Example 1, Nagra 3.142). Clearly in a rough state, with some missing lyrics and several poor guitar fills from Lennon, we hear the following musical event in the transitional spot: a repeated, descending bass line from the D tonic (D, C sharp, B, A) to the A dominant pitches. This is a logical structure to include in a song that emulates an earlier popular song style, as the bass resembles an upright (pizzicato) bass pattern moving from tonic to the dominant – for instance, suggesting Irving Berlin's 'Steppin' Out with My Baby', with its descending bass. But it is apparent that the group is not familiar with the main elements of the song, since the rehearsal breaks down and the remainder of the 14-minute track is spent trying to find the right drum beat and learning the chords. This descending bass line would return in a later rehearsal.

The second interlude attempt is more interesting and is even given a name during the sessions. This musical pattern is rehearsed several times and seemed to be a McCartney favourite (Audio Examples 2 and 3, Nagra 3.143 and 3.144). After the lyric 'made sure that Joan was dead', McCartney draws out the word 'dead' and plays a short progression over an A pedal, the dominant of the song. The progression, made up of an A major chord, moving to a Dm/A, to an A7 and back is a short neighbouring gesture that builds tension over the pedal point and sustained vocal. After the first performance of this transition, McCartney labels it 'dead music' in relation to the lyric and makes an off-mic reference to it being something that occurs in movies. Subsequent takes include the 'dead music' in rehearsals, where McCartney tries to show Lennon the chords several times, but Lennon has trouble finding them on the guitar. The transition is also proposed as the introduction at some points in the discussion.

Still not happy with the interlude/intro, later that day (3 January) the Beatles tried shifting the duple metre into triple metre, in the style of a waltz (Audio Example 4, Nagra 3.150). This change occurs over a tonic and dominant alternation, infused with a particularly irritating tone from Harrison's bass ploddingly plunking out the chord roots. McCartney forgets the lyrics for most of the verses, and generally sloppy playing — including another poor guitar solo from Lennon — mars the attempt at this new approach. However, the group sound as though they are having fun, laughing and joking between takes, and working to incorporate the waltz idea into the song. This was the last version of 'Maxwell' recorded on 3 January, and the group would not seriously rehearse the tune again until 7 January. Apparently these four days in between changed McCartney's mind, because after playing it on 7 January he states that he does not like the waltz. Amusingly, Starr jokes that the waltz feel is the only thing he remembered about the whole song.

The descending bass, 'dead music' and waltz now discarded, on the evening of 7 January the Beatles move next to interlude 4, which is the simplest structurally of the transitions tried for 'Maxwell' (Audio Example 5, Nagra 7.56). Again, attempting to find an interlude that would both serve the song harmonically, emphasizing the dominant as the verse returns, and create tension for that return, McCartney plays four bars of an augmented triad in quarter notes while he 'aahs' over it. Though not particularly groundbreaking, interlude 4 features a connection to the song that follows it on the finished album, 'Oh! Darling', in its chordal similarity. Another McCartney-penned song, 'Oh! Darling' begins on an augmented chord and was also rehearsed on the same days as 'Maxwell'. The instability of the augmented chord, clearly in McCartney's musical consciousness at the time, seemed like a good possibility for building tension on the dominant. However, this interlude was quickly jettisoned in favour of no. 1, back to the jaunty descending bass line. McCartney appears willing to experiment with anything at this point to fill the space.

With the return to interlude no. 1 in later sessions on 7 January, the Beatles add the whistling that made it into the *Let It Be* movie (interlude no. 5, Audio Example 6, Nagra 7.58). On one track, McCartney performs a whistle solo over the verse, while Lennon plays some guitar fills. When it breaks down, McCartney indicates that he wants a 'real whistle solo' over the verse that then leads into the interlude with the descending bass line over the tonic D chord. Harrison, playing bass, suggests that they make the interlude more harmonically active. He suggests a progression of D, F sharp minor, G, A (I–iii–IV–V) to lead back into the verse and demonstrates it on the bass while McCartney listens. But this suggestion is dismissed when McCartney returns to the descending bass line idea and ponders whether Harrison and Starr should drop out altogether. Though not eventually chosen, this discussion reveals how the other members made attempts to contribute to the song.

Later that day, the group turn the interlude into the introduction, with three whistlers singing descending scale degrees 1, 7, 6, 5 over the repeated D major triad in the piano, without Starr's beat. Each interlude repeats this same progression, although the whistling is sometimes embellished. By this point Mal Evans has been recruited to play the anvil, and the song more closely resembles the eventual completed version. This fusion of interlude no. 1 with the whistling lends a spirited feel, where one might envision seeing a group of children skipping down the street. The whistle intro/transition would survive for the rest of the *Get Back* sessions intact, despite 'Maxwell' still not having a proper third verse, and despite Harrison's abrupt departure from the group on 10 January 1969. After Harrison left that day, the other Beatles (plus Yoko Ono) tried to regroup and play through 'Maxwell', but the session devolved into a competition between Lennon and McCartney to see who could perform the silliest version of the song: McCartney starred as a drunk, and Lennon sang with a faux-German accent. And with that, the song was shelved until July 1969 when it reappeared for consideration on *Abbey Road*.

## *Abbey Road* sessions

When the band regrouped that summer, McCartney had finally finished the lyrics and the rest of the Beatles were on their best behaviour — except for Lennon. The day the Beatles reconvened to record 'Maxwell' was the infamous session when Lennon and Ono returned from their car accident in Scotland, and a bed was wheeled into EMI to allow Ono to recuperate comfortably in the confines of Studio Two. Lennon flatly refused to participate on 'Maxwell', and thus the final version of the song became a McCartney, Harrison and Starr production, with help from Martin (organ).[8] This is particularly ironic because Lennon expressed extensive rancour regarding 'Maxwell', exaggerating the amount of recording time taken, and the cost and effort spent working on it. And for all that apparent unhappiness, he did not even play on the final version.

By this point, McCartney had structured the interlude in its final form (Audio Example 7, interlude no. 6). Take 5 from the 9 July session, released on *Anthology 3*, shows how much the group had progressed in their musicianship since January. This version presents the core of the song without the Moog, guitar and vocal overdubs. In this form, the interlude is still used as the introduction, with the addition of a drum fill, but now featuring a 'slick' harmonic progression of D — F sharp$^7$/C sharp — Bm — D/A, G, D, or in Roman numerals in the key of D major, I — V$^{4/3}$ of vi — vi

---

8. Howlett (2019: 31) notes that Mal Evans missed these sessions to reprise adding the initial anvil part from January 1969, so it was played by Ringo Starr on the finished version.

— I$^{6/4}$ (passing) — IV — I (Everett 1999: 252). As explained earlier, this music is not completely new, because it is built on the descending bass line that appeared numerous times in the *Get Back* sessions as interlude no. 1. However, in keeping with McCartney's increasingly sophisticated sense of harmony, on full display in the *Abbey Road* medley, the use of the applied chord (V$^{4/3}$ of vi) remains a striking touch, as does the quasi-plagal cadence (IV-I) hinted at before the return to the verse. Additionally, a new applied chord is formed in the final version when the Moog synthesizer adds the chordal seventh on the fourth chord, making a V$^{4/3}$ of IV (D7/A), creating a mini chain of applied V$^{4/3}$ chords. Of course, the introduction/interlude was excised from the final version of the song, which begins immediately with the first verse.

The 2019 *Abbey Road* anniversary edition adds take 12 from 9 July, when the song's structure had developed a bit further. McCartney leads the three Beatles (minus Lennon) through the rehearsal, having a lot of fun with the lyrics and telling the others that they should keep the 'nice bits' they play in the song. The introduction is still retained as the interlude, which would not change until later, and everything else is in its final place except for the Moog.

The official version on *Abbey Road* serves as the final product of experimentation, rearranged interludes and added surreal musical touches. The 2019 remix created and produced by Giles Martin significantly amplifies the Moog part, doubling the piano part in the first interlude, as well as the countermelody in verse 2.[9] Pertaining to the interludes, McCartney arpeggiates the 'slick' chords in a quasi-classical fashion after the guitar solo, preceding the third verse; this technique produces more directed, driving motion in the interlude towards the final verse (Audio Example 8).

---

9. This link isolates the Moog synthesizer part: https://www.youtube.com/watch?v=UQXD_G6RI3k (accessed 18 April 2024).

## Conclusions

What does this search for the perfect transition for those four bars in 'Maxwell's Silver Hammer' reveal, considering the disdain expressed for the song by both critics and those involved? I would argue three points. First, as notable people such as Giles Martin and Peter Jackson have described and shown, the atmosphere in the *Get Back* sessions certainly had its tense and difficult moments, but on the numerous takes examined here there was no particular grumbling or complaining from the other Beatles about 'Maxwell's Silver Hammer', except when someone could not play his part correctly or remember the chords (*Beatlefan* 2021: 16–17). In fact, evidence from the first day of 'Maxwell' rehearsals in the *Get Back* movie (3 January) reveals the Beatles' resilience and the apparently welcome opportunity to work on the song after a particularly difficult conversation. The group had been discussing venues for the live show with director Michael Lindsay-Hogg and others, and could not come up with a consensus. Harrison, growing more exasperated, suggests that the group get a 'divorce', which McCartney seconds, saying that he proposed that 'at the last meeting'. To defuse the tension, Lindsay-Hogg proposes that the group play for a while, and so they launch into McCartney teaching them 'Maxwell'. For the next several minutes in the film (1:13:50–1:17:30), we see the Beatles goofing around, smiling, doing the whistling parts, and the segment concludes with McCartney asking Mal Evans to get a hammer and an anvil, which we then see Evans playing in a run-through. Either the Beatles were happy to play anything to escape the prior weighty conversation, or they really were enjoying themselves playing 'Maxwell', a song that gave them the chance to perform in a lighthearted style. Evidence from the sessions would lean towards the latter explanation.

Second, and building on the prior point, we also hear the Beatles collaborating and offering different suggestions to McCartney, who, even though he had a clear idea of how the song was to be played, at least considered these at face value. To McCartney, the path from the descending bass line in interlude no. 1 to the final chordal progression needed to move through the various other forms until the group landed on the right one.

And finally, this sequence of sessions and an intense focus on one song illuminates how McCartney's musical mind was so productive that he could almost not stop playing, singing or writing in the studio while the others had trouble keeping up. With Lennon distracted from the group by drugs and his burgeoning relationship with Yoko Ono, Starr not participating in the creative aspects of the *Get Back* sessions when the heart of this song was developed, and Harrison trying but playing a different instrument than his normal one (bass), McCartney steps up and owns this song. Even in *Lyrics*, he acknowledges some of the challenges involved with the song's recording, but must have been pleased enough with the results because it was chosen for that selective book. And the song continues to inspire creative and clever criticisms, including this barb from Jonathan Gould:

> The sorriest aspect of 'Maxwell's Silver Hammer' is thus the way it demonstrates how Paul's workmanlike tendency to build on his past successes had caused him to translate the genuinely charming novelty and subversive parody of 'When I'm Sixty-Four' into a personal subgenre of glibly clever songs that had devolved in the two years since *Sgt. Pepper* into a form of musical schtick. (Gould 2007: 579)

One may love or hate McCartney's pastiche songs, but I believe he must be given credit for believing in his work at a time when his colleagues were not completely engaged. Additionally, the surreal aspects of the song's lyrics, story and music would become even more pronounced throughout McCartney's solo career, where he displayed a penchant for experimentation and unconventional sources of inspiration. In this regard, McCartney's development and growth as a songwriter becomes even more apparent, and I would argue, more impressive.

The title of this article comes from a quotation from George Harrison referring to McCartney's leadership on 'Maxwell's Silver Hammer', stating that 'after a while we did a good job on it, but when Paul got an idea or an arrangement in his head...' (*Crawdaddy Magazine* 1977). Although Harrison expresses his frustration at

McCartney's working methods, it is clear they led to the Beatles producing one of their most polished musical productions on *Abbey Road*.

## Bibliography

*Beatlefan* (2021) 'Q&A: Giles Martin, on updating "Let It Be" for the 21st century', *Beatlefan* 252: 16–17.

Bergstrom, John (2009) 'The "worst" of the Beatles: a contradiction in terms?', *PopMatters*, 12 November, https://www.popmatters.com/115700-the-worst-of-the-beatles-a-contradiction-in-terms-2496119956.html (accessed 18 April 2024).

Bök, Christian (2002) *'Pataphysics: The Poetics of an Imaginary Science* (Evanston, IL: Northwestern University Press).

Burr, Charles (1998) *Ealing Studios*, 3rd edn (Berkeley: University of California Press).

Corbyn, Zoë (2005) 'An introduction to 'Pataphysics', *The Guardian*, 9 December, https://www.theguardian.com/culture/2005/dec/09/8 (accessed 18 April 2024).

*Crawdaddy Magazine* (1977) 'George Harrison Interview: *Crawdaddy Magazine*, February 1977', Beatles Interviews Database, http://www.beatlesinterviews.org/db1977.0200.beatles.html (accessed 20 August 2022).

Emerick, Geoff and Howard Massey (2006) *Here, There and Everywhere: My Life Recording the Music of the Beatles* (New York: Gotham Books).

Everett, Walter (1999) *The Beatles as Musicians: Revolver through the Anthology* (New York: Oxford University Press).

Gould, Jonathan (2007) *Can't Buy Me Love: The Beatles, Britain, and America* (New York: Three Rivers Press).

Howlett, Kevin (2019) 'Track by Track', liner notes for *Abbey Road, Anniversary Edition*, Apple Records, 30–31.

Jackson, Peter (dir.) (2021) *The Beatles: Get Back*.

MacDonald, Ian (2005) *Revolution Inside Your Head: The Beatles' Records and the Sixties*, 3rd edn (Chicago: Chicago Review Press).

McCartney, Paul and Paul Muldoon (2021) *The Lyrics, 1956 to the Present* (New York: Liveright).

Miles, Barry (1997) *Paul McCartney: Many Years from Now* (New York: Henry Holt).
Riley, Tim (1988) *Tell Me Why: The Beatles, Album by Album, Song by Song, the Sixties and After* (New York: Alfred A. Knopf).
Skaggs, Austin (2018) 'Ringo Starr talks "Liverpool 8," the sixties, being overly medicated during Beatles gigs: exclusive audio', *Rolling Stone*, 25 June.
Sulpy, Doug and Ray Schweighart (1997) *Get Back: The Unauthorized Chronicle of the Beatles' Let It Be Disaster* (New York: St Martin's Press).
Thurmaier, David (2023) '"Shall we dance? This is fun!": Paul McCartney's popular song pastiches', in *The Beatles and Humour: Mockers, Funny Papers, and Other Play* (New York: Bloomsbury), pp. 133–150.
Womack, Kenneth (2019) *Solid State: The Story of Abbey Road and the End of the Beatles* (Ithaca, NY: Cornell University Press).
Womack, Kenneth (2023) *Living the Beatles Legend: The Untold Story of Mal Evans* (New York: HarperCollins).

## Audio files

I have included the Nagra files referenced in the text at this link: https://drive.google.com/drive/folders/1UPLJtc8hLw_IRuCCINjydeV-web99eOI?usp=share_link

# Carry that weight
## Entrepreneurial teams, creativity and conflict in the Beatles

Nick Williams
*Leeds University Business School, Clarendon Road, Leeds LS2 9NG*
*N.E.Williams@leeds.ac.uk*

**Abstract:** This article examines creativity and conflict in the Beatles. Building on the theory of entrepreneurial teams, the article shows that even in the most creative group settings, leadership is required to sustain creativity over time. Initially, restless determination and creativity can compensate for a lack of leadership, but eventually an absence of leadership can mean that conflict is not resolved. The pre-Epstein Beatles years can be characterized as lacking real organizational leadership, but this was compensated for by drive and the focal point of de facto leader John. The Epstein years brought strategic direction and leadership, while the post-Epstein years saw a disintegration of leadership, with others, particularly Paul, trying to fill the gap after Epstein's death. In the end, entrepreneurial teams cannot sustain their creativity without effective leadership. Evidence from the Beatles' career, particularly the *Get Back* sessions, is used to demonstrate how leadership is required, even among highly creative groups.

**Keywords:** entrepreneurial teams, creativity, conflict, leadership

This article examines entrepreneurial teams and the importance of leadership in the creative setting of the Beatles. An entrepreneurial team can be defined as a group of people with a common goal that can only be achieved by appropriate combinations of individual entrepreneurial actions (Harper 2008). Most often, entrepreneurial teams are studied in the context of a narrow definition of entrepreneurship, namely focused on business start-up and/or growth. Yet a broad definition of entrepreneurship also encompasses aspects such as creativity and innovation (Huggins and Williams 2009). Often these can be applied to firm settings, but at the same time the study of entrepreneurship can learn from other fields, including the arts, where creative entrepreneurship takes place. Creative entrepreneurship can be defined as the entrepreneurial process of creative-design and creative-artistic entrepreneurs (Leick et al. 2023), with creative entrepreneurs drawing on their artistic and creative sensibility to identify opportunities and provide creative products, services or experience (Chang and Chen 2020).

The article focuses on such creative entrepreneurship in a team setting: the Beatles. The lens of entrepreneurial teams allows new insights to be developed which show how leadership is important in creative group settings, and that without it the team will become dysfunctional and ultimately disband. The Beatles were active as a group between 1960 and 1970 and were a creative group of musicians and also a business. The creative journey of the group is often examined as a success, eclipsing music groups that went before and have existed since (Sunstein 2022). As Lewisohn (2013) states, they are the genuine ultimate, both in terms of musical contributions and commercial success. Being a popular musician has always involved business dimensions (Haynes and Marshall 2018), and the Beatles' business operations have influenced countless people in the creative industries and beyond. Under the management of Brian Epstein from 1962 until his death in 1967, they became more business minded (McNab 2015), exploiting various commercial opportunities while increasing their creative output. This continued after Epstein's death, and after returning from India in 1968 they were, in John Lennon's words, 'ready to play businessman' (Slate 2020). Apple Corps was founded to handle the Beatles' business interests after accountants informed the group that they had £2 million that they could invest in a business or lose to the Inland Revenue in taxation, and the firm is still in operation today (Perry 2009). It was Apple that provided the communication that signalled the end of the Beatles. Apple issued a press release on 10 April 1970, announcing that 'spring is here and Leeds play Chelsea tomorrow and Ringo and John and George and Paul are alive and well and full of hope' (Rachel 2021). Despite the upbeat nature of the release, it effectively announced the end of the group, with Paul McCartney later filing for dissolution of the Beatles' contractual partnership on 31 December 1970, which was finalized formally in 1974 after years of legal disputes. Business dealings would ultimately get in the way of the creative element of the band, and without the leadership of Epstein conflict would arise and not be adequately resolved.

Through the lens of entrepreneurial teams, a new understanding of the demise of the Beatles is possible. This article shows how the end of the Beatles was not simply the result of business dealings and personal animosities which emerged during their final years together. Rather, it examines how the different phases of their career as a group, from team formation, through effective collaboration and team dissolution, all contributed to ensuring the end. This study posits that this was a matter of leadership, which was effective for years under Brian Epstein's management but could not replicated after his death.

This article examines how entrepreneurial teams can enhance individual creativity and how creativity can be enhanced in entrepreneurial teams. It also examines how creativity can be stifled depending on internal and external contexts. The article shows that the pre-Epstein Beatles years can be characterized as lacking real organizational leadership, but this was compensated for by the drive and focal point of de facto leader John. Drawing on the Epstein years of the Beatles, the article shows that managers are needed to harness individual creativity as well as that of the group. Management was important in the Epstein years, and indeed managers are important in all organizational settings (Foss and Klein 2022). The Epstein period led to increased organization of the group, increased access to commercial opportunities as well as critical success. The post-Epstein years saw a disintegration of leadership, with John increasingly distracted from the Beatles' creative output, and Paul assuming leadership responsibilities until Allen Klein was appointed as manager, despite not being fully accepted by the group. In the end, this leadership could not be sustained and conflict arose about the direction and activities of the group and who should, or should not, be leading. This demonstrates that leadership was important throughout the career of the Beatles, and it was not just the artistic endeavours of the group and their eventual disharmony that led to the band's dissolution.

The argument makes the following contributions to Beatles research. First, it shows that leadership is required to coordinate work (Foss and Klein 2022), and this is important in creative group settings. Although creative individuals can be autonomous, groups require leadership to ensure that creative talents can be harnessed and fulfilled. Second, it shows that without effective leadership, conflict can emerge and often will not be resolved. Conflict resolution is a key leadership skill but requires a leader in place to do it (Mohan 2022). This means that while creativity can burn brightly, it cannot be sustained over the long term. Divisions become more pronounced without management in place, eventually leading to the dissolution of even the most productive creative group settings. This brings new insights to analysis of the Beatles, as their dissolution was not just created by arguments and resentment in the later years, but was in fact a result of decisions made throughout their career.

I begin by briefly setting out the literature on entrepreneurial teams, and how this can be useful for examining groups in highly creative settings. I then examine the role of entrepreneurial teams in the pre-Epstein years, showing how restless musicianship secured success, but that in lacking real leadership formal success through record contracts and chart entries was elusive. The importance of leadership in the Epstein years is then discussed, demonstrating the importance of increasing the focus and commercial viability of the group. The post-Epstein years are then examined, which can be characterized as lacking real management of the group, despite the later involvement of Allen Klein, and increasing tensions and conflict. The conclusion presents a number of implications for understanding entrepreneurial teams in creative settings, and how the Beatles provide lessons for other forms of entrepreneurial teams.

## Understanding entrepreneurial teams in creative settings

Entrepreneurship research has tended to privilege the individual. Shane and Venkataraman (2000) emphasized the nexus of lucrative opportunities and enterprising individuals, while Schumpeter developed the notion of the 'lone hero' with exceptional creative ability who overcomes all barriers to launch new innovations (Harper 2008). Yet this ignores the fact that entrepreneurship is often a team effort (Cooney 2005; Klotz et al. 2013).

An entrepreneurial team can be defined as a group of entrepreneurs with a common goal that can only be achieved by appropriate combinations of individual entrepreneurial actions (Harper 2008). Entrepreneurial team members hold an ownership position and are motivated to utilize their human capital to benefit the group's performance and growth (Tihula et al. 2009). To operate effectively, entrepreneurial teams need to apply rules such as shared goals, complementary skills, commitment to a common purpose and an approach that holds individuals mutually accountable (Katzenbach and Smith 2008). Entrepreneurial teams can differ in terms of their size, how the team members are arranged within the team, how authority to make decisions is determined and how the team communicate with each other (Harper 2008). Entrepreneurial teams also differ from organizational teams, in that they have undefined social rules, teams roles are ambiguous, and the organization is evolving (De Mol et al. 2015). This means that greater strategic freedom can provoke problems in team cohesion and decision-making processes (Preller et al. 2016).

All entrepreneurs apply creativity in some form, and creativity in entrepreneurship is discernible in processes such as the creation of new ventures and new products and identifying new markets. However, creativity takes on a new dimension when the creative aspect is a central force that is embodied by the person (Patten and Stephens 2023). Entrepreneurial teams cannot sustain creative outputs indefinitely. While the motivation of members of the team prompts them to invest efforts that benefit the venture, debating and discussing decisions, if leadership lacks clarity or is not shared then conflict can arise (Schjoedt and Kraus 2009). Divergent visions can also lead to friction (Preller et al. 2020). Drazin et al. (1999) show that periodic organizational crises inevitably entail contradictions and tensions. This means that group members change their shared frames of reference and collective belief structures towards renewed shared understandings of what activities are deemed creative (Thompson 2018). A lack of team cohesion means that members' satisfaction decreases (Chen et al. 2017), ultimately rendering the team unviable. Understanding conflict in an entrepreneurial team is of significant importance because the quality of decisions in an entrepreneurial team has a direct effect on the team's sustainability (Amason 1996). With a lack of leadership, conflicts can remain unresolved. This can be particularly true in the creative industries, where leadership and creativity are complex, with artists reconciling very different, even contradictory, ways of thinking (Bilton 2013).

While much of the literature on entrepreneurial teams focuses on business venture creation, by taking a broader definition of entrepreneurship which encompasses creativity it is possible to view other forms of organization through this prism. Creativity is a facet of all entrepreneurial action, but has particular meaning in the context of creative industries (Patten and Stephens 2023). As with other creative entrepreneurs, the Beatles embodied the product they provided as well as being the exploiters of the opportunity. The Beatles were a 'business' in a broad sense. Yet it is their creativity, imagination and innovation in music which best defines them. In this sense they can be viewed as entrepreneurial (Staley 2020). The Beatles were creative entrepreneurs in that they provided symbolic content that required artistic creativity as quintessentially knowledge-based, culture-driven and artistry-intensive labour input (Chang and Chen 2020). By drawing on the theory of entrepreneurial teams, it is possible to analyse how their creativity was harnessed and how, in the end, it could not be sustained.

# Examining entrepreneurial teams and creativity through the Beatles

The journey of the Beatles can be seen as distinct phases, which Duffett (2023) terms early development, Beatlemania, post-Beatlemania and post-Beatles. This article takes a similar view and focuses on three phases: team formation in the pre-Epstein years, team collaboration during the Epstein years and team dissolution in the post-Epstein period. This reflects the fact that entrepreneurial teams undergo a life cycle, in that teams are born, mature and eventually dissolve. This approach provides a useful framing for understanding the role of leadership and management in entrepreneurial teams, and complements the view of the creative process being at the heart of the Beatles (Clydesdale 2010). Figure 1 provides a visual overview of the life-cycle phases and the key elements of team formation, along with illustrative examples of the life cycle of the Beatles' journey.

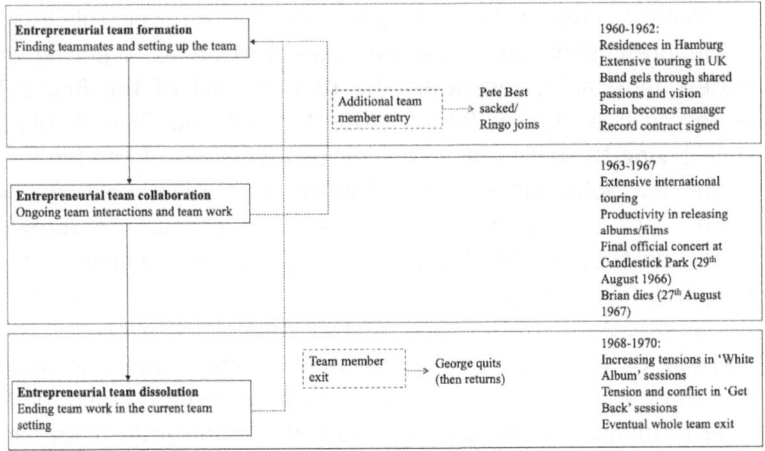

Figure 1. The entrepreneurial team life cycle and the Beatles journey (life cycle adapted from Patzelt et al. 2021)

## *Team formation: the pre-Epstein years*

The life of an entrepreneurial team begins when an individual recruits other members or when a group of individuals starts to develop an opportunity (Lazar et al. 2020). The team formation phase is the time during which the team members find each other, agree to form a team, and set up the team's structure, and is guided to a large extent by the self-selection of team members (Patzelt et al. 2021).

The story of the Beatles' team formation is well known, from Paul meeting John at the Woolton Village Fete, to Paul bonding with George on the school bus over their love of music and inviting him to meet John. This meant that the team was self-selected, and the three would begin to play together, even without a distinct opportunity in mind. John was the de facto leader having formed the Quarry Men, and was fretting over his own leadership or whether to make the group stronger by inviting Paul to join (Norman 2005). Paul and George (and later Ringo) deferred to him in matters of strategic direction (Lewisohn 2013), and this continued throughout the Beatles' career, with John's leadership status never truly lost.

The pre-Epstein years can be characterized as a period of restless musicality, recreating the rock 'n' roll of the Beatles' heroes such as Chuck Berry, Little Richard and Elvis Presley, while trying to strike out with their own versions of the big hits of the day. John and Paul would write songs together at Paul's house, approaching creation with a sense of purpose (Brown 2021), and they would play whatever gigs were available. After struggling to secure paying gigs in their home city of Liverpool, the band took off to Germany. At this stage of their career, the intensity of the work schedule was an element in their team formation. Residencies in Hamburg quickly gelled the group, both as performing musicians and personally (Lewisohn 2013). They had to satisfy demanding club promoters and entertain demanding audiences. This period was not without management per se. Allan Williams had helped the group secure bookings in Hamburg as well as the UK, including a residency at the Indra Club for which they recruited Pete Best, as they were lacking a permanent drummer. Williams's management was not destined to last, and after an argument about his 10 per cent commission the Beatles parted ways with him.

In this early phase of their career, shared (or team) cognition (Chen et al. 2017; Patzelt et al. 2021) was strengthened. This is important as it binds team members together in the early stages of activity (Chen et al. 2017) and can occur without effective or defined leadership in place. Shared cognition manifests in how well team members understand each other, by sharing the same goals. In pseudo-American accents, the group would ask of John: 'Where we going, Johnny?', to which he would reply 'To the toppermost of the poppermost' (Lewisohn 2013: 364). Shared cognition also plays a vital role in increasing a team's cohesion. Team cohesion, which embodies the closeness of a team to each other and their commitment to the team, benefits entrepreneurial team performance because there are fewer process losses and better member coordination (Ensley et al. 2002). Team cohesion was built during these early years performing in Hamburg, although the final line-up of the group was not yet secured.

### The collaboration phase: the Epstein years

Once an entrepreneurial team has formed, it enters the collaboration phase. The collaboration phase is the period during which an entrepreneurial team, based on its current composition and structure, interacts to develop opportunities together (Patzelt et al. 2021). While entrepreneurial teams can be seen as cases of self-management, with freedom and discretion and the ability to organize their internal work and structure (Langfred 2007), as a team grows and develops, more active leadership may be required (Patzelt et al. 2021). Thus, the Beatles turned to Brian Epstein.

Inviting Epstein to manage the group was based on the group's understanding of what was best for them, an understanding that they needed a manager and more effective leadership than they had previously had (Lewisohn 2013). Epstein was invited to manage the group during discussions in late 1961, and the Beatles signed a contract for him to manage them on 24 January 1962 (Lewisohn 2013). This was despite Epstein not having music industry experience. He ran the music department of his family's business and happened to hear the Beatles at a lunchtime session at the Cavern (Brown 2021). He liked what he saw and heard: 'I was immediately struck by their music, their beat and their sense of humour on stage ... And even afterward, when I met them, I was struck again by their personal charm and it was there that it all started' (Lewisohn 2013: 517).

Despite Epstein's lack of music industry knowledge and experience, he provided the leadership which had been lacking. His management and drive can be exemplified through his efforts to get the Beatles signed to a record label. Epstein faced significant doubts from record companies, most notably Decca, whose head Dick Rowe apparently stated that 'groups of guitarists are on their way out' (Lewisohn 2013: 578). No one at these early record company meetings thought they were a team of creative geniuses (Clydesdale 2010). However, despite record company indifference, Epstein remained determined (Mohan 2022), and responded that he was completely confident that one day they would be bigger than Elvis Presley (Epstein 1964). Ultimately, George Martin, who would later become the Beatles' producer and was at the time an A&R manager of EMI's Parlophone label, was convinced by Epstein's faith in 'the boys' and offered them a recording contract after some initial reservations (Lewisohn 2013).

Epstein's effective leadership also meant that the group could withstand early setbacks and challenges. Due to the shared cognition built up during the early years of extensive touring, it was possible for the Beatles to withstand the exit of a team member. Pete Best undoubtedly played a role in the early phase of the Beatles as they honed their craft, but he left before the true creative phase, which involved the development of songwriting skills. The team withstood this early team member exit. As Patzelt et al. (2021) have noted, we do not know how teams in the early phases coordinate their composition in terms of potential members they do not wish to include. However, the story of the Beatles provides a good illustration of how this can be managed. The sacking of Best was one of Epstein's early decisive moves, although he had been cajoled by the Beatles to do it. The Beatles had performed a number of gigs with Ringo Starr when Best had been ill, and they enjoyed his drumming as well as his company. As Paul commented, 'It had got to the stage that Pete was holding us back. What were we going to do — try and pretend he was a wonderful drummer?' (Lewisohn 2013: 677). Unwilling to deal with the emotional side of sacking Best, they went to Epstein and said 'You're the manager, you do it' (Lewisohn 2013: 677). Best was summoned to Epstein's office on 16 August 1962 and told that the boys wanted him out and Ringo in (Best and Doncaster 2001). This illustrates the importance of the manager taking the decisive action, but also how the search for a replacement had already taken place, meaning that the impact of the team member's exit could be minimized. When Ringo joined on 18 August 1962 the shared cognition of the band was enhanced further. Now they had a group who all were happy with, and who were all moving in the same direction. This meant that they could better share individual abilities with the group, provide shared representations, interpretations, mutual goals and a system of meaning, key features of shared cognition (Nahapiet and Ghoshal 1998).

With the band settled under his leadership, the restless, leather-jacketed, pre-Epstein days were gone. In came suits as a sign of professionalism and uniformity (Staley 2020) and effective management. Epstein provided the group with the organization required to make it to the 'toppermost of the poppermost' (Lewisohn 2013: 364). Epstein drove the band forward in terms of recording contracts, merchandising, film making, publishing and many other commercial opportunities. Under Epstein's management the Beatles saw success such as no band had previously experienced and none since has truly emulated. The band released their debut album *Please Please Me* in 1963, and this was followed by *With the Beatles* (1963), *A Hard Day's Night* (1964), *Beatles for Sale* (1964), *Help* (1965), *Rubber Soul* (1965), *Revolver* (1966) and *Sgt. Pepper's Lonely Hearts Club Band* (1967), along with the films *A Hard's Day Night* (1964) and *Help* (1965). The Beatles' output was unprecedented in terms of innovation and productivity during Epstein's management. Clydesdale (2010) has argued that while Epstein was open to their creativity, none of his practices had an impact on that creativity. Yet it was a product of the freedom that he enabled the band to have. The band were able to focus on honing their craft as musicians and the creative element of their output, rather than organizing gigs and attempting to secure record contracts.

The Epstein years were not, of course, without tensions and conflict. The group became increasingly frustrated with touring, and angry with Epstein for insisting on what they regarded as an exhausting schedule (Spitz 2005). The intensity of a work schedule can mean that close interactions have a high potential for engendering conflicts within teams (Forbes, Korsgaard and Sapienza 2010). The Beatles were tired of touring almost constantly and had become weary of performing concerts at which the screaming was often so loud that it drowned out the music (Duffett 2023). The last Beatles concert at Candlestick Park on 29 August 1966 meant that Epstein's role was going to change. It is also fair to say that his decision making had not always proved exemplary. He had licensed the Beatles' name and likeness for merchandise, stating that he would accept a penny less than 10 per cent, despite the typical range being 30–50 per cent. This decision cost the Beatles in lost royalties and when the royalty agreement was eventually renegotiated Beatlemania was on the wane (Greathouse 2015). Over time, Epstein had become increasingly worried that the group, particularly Paul, were discontented with his management, and made strenuous efforts to prove to the group that they still needed him (Norman 2005).

## Team dissolution: the post-Epstein years

The dissolution phase is the period during which one, several or all team members leave an entrepreneurial team, such that the team discontinues its joint work on the venture (Patzelt et al. 2021). The post-Epstein years can be seen as a gradual dissolution. The band was ageing and becoming less passionate about remaining Beatles. Yet a significant factor in this dissolution was also the lack of effective leadership to resolve the increasing tensions and conflict.

Brian Epstein died on 27 August 1967, three months after the release of *Sgt. Pepper's Lonely Hearts Club Band*. In the early post-Epstein period, the Beatles struck a rich vein of creativity, moving from *Sgt. Pepper* through *Magical Mystery Tour*, *The Beatles*

(*The White Album*), *Let it Be* and *Abbey Road*. Despite this, this phase also marked a period of tensions rising, falling and rising again, with the restless creativity of the band being marshalled by its members, often Paul, and a string of hangers-on, lawyers and new management (McNab 2015). However, none of these, together or alone, could replicate the management of Epstein and the willingness of the band to operate under delegated leadership.

The cracks had begun to show during the *White Album* sessions in 1968 (Staley 2020). A creative outcome of the increased tension was the evidence of the individual tastes of each member of the Beatles coming more to the fore (DeRosa 2020). The *White Album* included the musique concrete of Lennon's 'Revolution 9', Ringo's country song 'Don't Pass Me By', Harrison's ballad 'While My Guitar Gently Weeps' and the stomping rock of Paul's 'Helter Skelter'. The album was individualistic by comparison with previous recordings (MacDonald 1994). John had lost interest in collaborating with Paul, and poured scorn on his efforts when the opportunity arose, describing 'Ob-La-Di, Ob-La-Da' as 'granny music shit' (Kapurch et al. 2023: 149). John had also introduced his new girlfriend, Yoko Ono, to the group, which created further tension given her attendance at recording sessions. Yoko's presence was regarded as intrusive and disruptive of the creative flow of the band (Staley 2020), as they had previously worked without the involvement of wives or girlfriends (Miles 1998). This had helped to establish the working culture of the band, and reflects how through effective management entrepreneurial teams can establish cultures that allow members to openly communicate and express individual passions (Ginting-Szczesny et al. 2023). This was made more difficult with Yoko sitting, often silently, beside John and contributing to the difficulties of the sessions (MacDonald 1994). In later years the *White Album* would be seen as the beginning of the end, with Paul stating that it 'wasn't a pleasant one to make', and he and John both seeing the sessions as the start of the band's demise (The Beatles 2000). The band's increasing individualism would be a key factor in their downfall. The *White Album* was released in November 1968, and sessions for the next album (later to be released as *Let It Be* in May 1970 as the Beatles' final album, despite being recorded before *Abbey Road*, released in September 1969) began in January 1969. It was at these sessions that tensions became even greater. The *Get Back* documentary brings many of these tensions to the fore, despite also showing a band still capable of brilliance and a desire to work through issues.

The *Get Back* sessions saw tensions mount and come to a head (Kapurch and Everett 2020), and showed a band aware of the lack of genuine management. While they were able to be productive and creative, the rot had begun to set in. As MacDonald (1994: 329) explains, 'the truth was that they were adults and no longer adaptable to the teenage gang mentality demanded by a functional pop/rock group'. The lack of leadership was bemoaned. George, for example, lamented how things had changed: 'Ever since Mr Epstein passed away, it's never been the same'; and Paul stated: 'There really is no one there now to say "do it", whereas there always used to be … but Daddy's gone away now and we are on our own.' In the face of the negativity, Paul tried to cajole the group: 'We've been very negative since Mr Epstein passed away and that's why all of us in turn have been sick of the group … It's discipline we lack.' In many ways, this was emblematic of the lack of leadership within the group. Paul had assumed leadership responsibilities, albeit reluctantly: 'I'm scared of … me being the boss. And I have been for, like, a couple of years — and we all have, you know, no pretending about that' (The Beatles 2021). In assuming this role, Paul created more tension and the group became more perturbed by his growing domination (Miles 1998). The *Get Back* sessions show George frustrated by Paul giving him and other band members instructions on what and how to play. For example, he says to Paul: 'I'll play whatever you want me to play, or I won't play at all if you don't want me to play … whatever it is that will please you, I'll do it' (The Beatles 2021). In situations where leadership is clear, team members accept that the leader has more power and dominance than themselves (Yin et al. 2020). However, the Beatles lacked this, and this is reflected in George's irritated response. They were not able to defer to a genuine leader to solve issues when conflict arose. The inability to resolve tensions was also not helped by John's descent into heroin addiction, which left him incommunicative and critical of the venture (Francis 2014).

Conflict in an entrepreneurial team is an inevitable social process that results from perceived incompatibilities between members (Chen 2006). The *Get Back* sessions contain numerous examples of low-level incompatibilities, with even seemingly minor decisions or disagreements taking greater significance. The Beatles started filming in Twickenham studios and there was disagreement about what the whole project actually was. A TV show is discussed, as well as a feature film and album, and a concert to provide a finale. Due to a lack of leadership, decisions are not made, or time is not allowed to gain everyone's tacit agreement, and conflicts remain unresolved. With no one prepared to be the real leader, and no manager in place, it falls to director Michael Lindsay-Hogg to try to push the band to make decisions, but with little impact. The disagreements highlight how the Beatles conform to two distinct forms of conflict: relationship conflict when there are interpersonal incompatibilities between team members, and task conflict, which occurs when there are disagreements regarding the content of the tasks that are being performed (Chen et al. 2017). Such disagreements can be generative, in that tension can lead to creative outputs. Indeed, despite the relationship conflict and task conflict in the *Get Back* sessions, the band still write, record and perform together. Positive conflicts create energy, while negative disputes detract from the creative output (Mohan 2022).

During *Get Back*, the Beatles are able to rally together to remain creative, making conflicts as positive as possible. However, a further element of the team dynamics which resulted from a lack of real leadership was how the need for achievement became more of a source of tension. Within teams, the perception of an individual's contribution can be a key source of contention (Khan et al. 2015). The need for achievement is particularly apparent in George in the *Get Back* film. As the youngest member of the band, George had always been treated as a 'junior' by Paul and John (Jones 2023). His frustration is part of the journey of the team. The journey of a team is emotional and highlights the important role of conflicts embedded in feelings and perceptions (Khan et al. 2015). George had often been frustrated by his perception of resistance from John and Paul to his contributions to albums, but this increased in the later years and is evidenced in *Get Back*. At a time when he is growing creatively, George is more uncomfortable with his secondary songwriting role, talking with John about how he could do a solo album based on all the songs he has written to fill his 'quota' for the Beatles for another decade. In a salient move, the band rehearse George's 'All Things Must Pass' but do not record it. This represents an emotional ambivalence towards George, and can be a feature of teams in which positive and negative emotions towards different passion foci increase team conflict (Ginting-Szczesny et al. 2023).

George's frustrations are not resolved and on 10 January 1969 he leaves the band, quietly announcing: 'I think I'll be ... I'm leaving.' John replies: 'What?' George: 'The band now' (The Beatles 2021). There then follows a discussion which highlights the lack of leadership, George suggesting that they write to the *NME* for a replacement, Mal Evans replying that he will speak to George Martin about money, and George saying, 'But he shouldn't be bothered with that ... That's why we've got Apple' (The Beatles 2021).

A key element in understanding the eventual dissolution of an entrepreneurial team is when a team member exits (Patzelt et al. 2021). In the case of the Beatles, George quitting in the middle of the *Get Back* sessions is illustrative. He wasn't the first person to quit the Beatles. Ringo had done so previously during the *White Album* sessions, forcing Paul to record the drum track for 'Back in the USSR' (MacDonald 1994: 310). Ringo was wooed back with charm: when he returned he found his drum kit decorated with flowers (Hertsgaard 1996). George quitting created more uncertainty precisely because the team was in a weaker position. As such, different responses to team exit emerge (Patzelt et al. 2021). The greater level of cohesion present when Ringo quit meant that creativity and understanding could be nurtured. However, when George quit there was less cohesion among the team, and affective conflict led to anger and alienation. This is exemplified in the lack of an initial strategy to get George to return to the group. At first the response is aimless, and the *Get Back* film shows Paul the day after George quits contemplating the uncertainty and looking emotionally vulnerable. Paul also tries to find humour in the situation, saying 'It's going to be such an incredible sort of comical thing like, in fifty years' time, you know: "They broke up because Yoko sat on an amp"' (The Beatles 2021).

A conversation recorded via a hidden microphone shows John and Paul well aware of their bandmate's lingering frustrations (Fisher 2022). They discuss whether George will return; John: 'It's been a festering wound ... and yesterday we allowed it to go even deeper, and we didn't give him any bandages'; Paul: 'I'm assuming he's coming back ... If he isn't then it's a new problem' (The Beatles 2021). John and Paul offer different reasons for George's frustrations. John says that Paul has silenced members of the group, is overbearing and has intimidated the other Beatles out of making musical suggestions, while Paul states that John has 'always been [the] boss' of the group (Fisher 2022: 246). Such emotional team relationship conflicts can be attributed to personal incompatibilities and to a divergence in perceptions, expectations and opinions (Khan et al. 2015). George quitting shows how relationship conflicts, which are person-related disagreements that include tension, animosity and annoyance among team members (Jehn 1995), become heightened without leadership to resolve them. In order to minimize the impacts of conflict, entrepreneurial teams must reconcile internal conflicts that could potentially hamper team cohesion and new venture performance (Chen et al. 2017). George quitting was symptomatic of the fact that the desire to remain in the group was waning, and that internal conflicts could not be resolved.

After George's departure, there were two band meetings and a six-day break to try to figure out a way forward. When George returned on 21 January the band had relocated to the more homely and welcoming basement of Apple's offices on Savile Row. There is also a new face at the sessions, Billy Preston, who the band had first met in Hamburg. Inviting guests was a means of cutting through tension and attempting to keep the group positively working together, an approach that had been taken before, with

Eric Clapton joining the 'While My Guitar Gently Weeps' recording for the *White Album*. At George's behest, discussions about a final concert to end the *Get Back* sessions are sidelined, but only in the short term. Paul, in particular, is still keen on the idea, believing in live performance as a source of creative energy (MacDonald 1994), as is Michael Lindsay-Hogg, and it re-emerges in conversation. There are numerous discussions regarding the location of the concert, to be filmed at the conclusion of the sessions. Several ideas are rejected, including a boat at sea (George: 'The idea of the boat is completely insane'), the Tunisian desert and the Colosseum. John at one point mutters: 'I'm warming to do it in an asylum' (MacDonald 1994: 329). Finally, the group settle on the rooftop of Apple Corps in Savile Row as a compromise (Staley 2020). This is despite George's initial resistance: 'I don't want to go on the roof' (The Beatles 2021: 189. However, after some cajoling the concert takes place, but weeks after the band had all but washed their hands of the entire project (Lewisohn 1992).

Although not on camera, the *Get Back* film hints at the introduction of Allen Klein, the manager of the Rolling Stones, to the group; he would eventually become John, George and Ringo's manager. John and Ringo discuss a meeting with Klein about taking over the Beatles' business, which foreshadows a bitter split with Paul. John is clearly impressed: 'I just think he's fantastic' (The Beatles 2021). Tensions had grown regarding the appointment of someone to manage the financial affairs of the Beatles, which had been lacking since Epstein's death. This remained unresolved following the conclusion of the *Get Back* sessions. Paul was in favour of appointing Lee and John Eastman, the father and brother of Linda, whom he married on 12 March 1969. However, John, George and Ringo favoured Klein. The group could not reach agreement, and as a result both Klein and the Eastmans were temporarily appointed, Klein as manager, while the Eastmans acted as their lawyers. Further conflict ensued until on 8 May Klein was named as the sole manager and the Eastmans were dismissed, despite Paul refusing to sign the contract. These disagreements would have long-term repercussions for the Beatles, with business contracts being a key source of dispute years after the band had split up.

Despite the tensions evident in the *Get Back* film, it is also important to note that it was also a highly creative and productive period, with many new tracks written, rehearsed and performed. In this sense, conflict can be seen as a catalyst for creativity and understanding as well as animosity and resentment, with effective teams embracing the benefits of conflict and avoiding its costs (Ensley et al. 2002). In the absence of effective leadership, the Beatles were unable to avoid the costs of conflict. Ultimately this would lead to the dissolution of the group.

While the *Get Back* sessions were not the last recordings by the Beatles, they signalled that the end was nigh. The Beatles rallied in order to record *Abbey Road*, which was released in September 1969. George Martin had been surprised to be invited by Paul to return to the recording studio, given that he viewed the *Get Back* sessions as a 'miserable experience' and 'thought that it was the end of the road for all of us' (Gould 2007: 560). The tensions continued at Abbey Road, with John rejecting Martin's proposal of a 'continuously moving piece of music', instead wanting his and Paul's songs to occupy separate sides of the album (Gould 2007). It would not be long after the release of *Abbey Road* that the group would split. This team exit represented the formal dissolution of the group; however, the end of the Beatles was not clean cut. All the members did not decide to leave at the same time. While John had said he was leaving, Paul was the first to formally announce that the band were no more. This would be followed by years of personal animosity and legal acrimony.

## Conclusion

And in the end, the Beatles became a worldwide sensation and succeeded where others had failed (Sunstein 2022). Their creative output was a process of continual improvement over time (Clydesdale 2010). However, the creativity of the group could not be sustained. The story of the Beatles shows that leadership and management are important. Authority and hierarchy are required in order to coordinate work, including creative outputs (Foss and

Klein 2022). Leaders can satisfy the competency, autonomy and emotional needs of team members and can strengthen the team culture to enhance mutual understanding (Yin et al. 2020).

The Epstein years brought effective leadership to the Beatles, which led to a period of unrivalled creativity and productivity. After Epstein's death, this leadership could not be replicated; there was no true successor who carried the credibility of having been there from the beginning (Jones and Podrazik 2022). With no one to carry the weight previously borne by Epstein, conflicts arose and were not resolved, which ultimately led to the dissolution of the group. When they arrived at the *Get Back* sessions, the gang mentality was lost, and while Paul was still determined to make things work, George was yearning to play guitar in an easy-going American band, Ringo was looking forward to being an actor, and John wanted to break the band mould and confront the world through cultural subversion in tandem with Yoko (MacDonald 1994). As Staley (2020) states, with hindsight the break-up of the Beatles was inevitable; the band was not artistically sustainable and art was the critical value that drove the enterprise.

It is possible for the members of cohesive teams to exhibit high levels of affinity and trust for one another as well as higher levels of satisfaction with and affective attraction to the group as a whole (Ensley et al. 2002). This can sustain a team for an extended period but cannot last forever. Indeed, the Beatles' affinity for each other and for what they were producing held them together in the team formation and team collaboration periods. From the early years of John and Paul honing their songwriting skills together, to the four members of the group producing a huge amount of highly creative and innovative output, this could not have been achieved without significant team harmony. The nature of the team was such that it possessed high levels of exchange and complementary blends of expertise and thinking styles (Clydesdale 2010). However, there are a variety of important paradoxes that seem fundamental to creativity in groups. One such paradox is the tension between freedom and constraint in the creative process (Rosso 2014). The Beatles had freedom to experiment and to explore new sounds and new ways of recording. As the personal relationships of the Fab Four grew more strained, their own musical tastes and artistic whims became more pronounced. Over time, this meant that their approach became more individualistic, meaning that they no longer needed the group as a creative outlet. In many ways, the strains and tensions at the heart of the Beatles' story helped to inform their creativity but would also lead to the group's demise.

## Acknowledgements

The author is grateful to Hannah Preston for valuable comments on an earlier version of this article.

## Bibliography

Amason, A. C. (1996) 'Distinguishing the effects of functional and dysfunctional conflict on strategic decision making: resolving a paradox for top management groups', *Academy of Management Journal* 39(1): 123–148.

The Beatles (2000) *The Beatles Anthology* (San Francisco: Chronicle Books).

The Beatles (2021) *The Beatles: Get Back* (London: Callaway).

Best, P. and P. Doncaster (2001) *Beatle! The Pete Best Story* (London: Plexus).

Bilton, Chris (2013) 'Playing to the gallery: myth, method and complexity in the creative process', in *Handbook of Research on Creativity*, ed. Kerry Thomas and Janet Chan (Cheltenham: Edward Elgar Publishing), 125–137.

Brown, C. (2021) *One two three four: The Beatles in Time* (London: Fourth Estate).

Chang, Y.-Y. and M.-H. Chen (2020) 'Creative entrepreneurs' creativity, opportunity recognition, and career success: is resource availability a double-edged sword?', *European Management Journal* 38: 750–762.

Chen, M.-H. (2006) 'Understanding the benefits and detriments of conflict on team creativity process', *Creativity and Innovation Management* 15(1): 105–116.

Chen, M.-H., Y.-Y. Chang and Y.-C. Chang (2017) 'The trinity of entrepreneurial team dynamics: cognition, conflicts and cohesion', *International Journal of Entrepreneurial Behavior & Research* 23(6): 934–951.

Clydesdale, G. (2010) 'Creativity and competition: The Beatles', *Creativity Research Journal* 18(2): 129–139.

Cooney, T. M. (2005) 'What is an entrepreneurial team?', *International Small Business Journal* 23(3): 226–235.

de Mol, E., S. N. Khapova and T. Elfring (2015) 'Entrepreneurial team cognition: a review', *International Journal of Management Reviews* 17(2): 232–255.

DeRosa, C. S. (2020) 'John Lennon out and in: "Revolution," the Beatles, and the Movement in 1968', *Rock Music Studies* 7(3): 199–208.

Drazin, R., M. A. Glynn and R. K. Kazanjian (1999) 'Multilevel theorizing about creativity in organizations: a sensemaking perspective', *Academy of Management Review* 24(2): 286–307.

Duffett, M. (2023) 'Reflections on Cass Sunstein's Beatlemania article: romantic behaviourialism?', *Journal of Beatles Studies* 2(1): 15–40.

Ensley, M. D., A. W. Pearson and A. C. Amason (2002) 'Understanding the dynamics of new venture top management teams: Cohesion, conflict, and new venture performance', *Journal of Business Venturing* 17(4): 365–386.

Epstein, B. (1964) *A Cellarful of Noise* (London: Souvenir Press).

Fisher, M. R. (2022) '*The Beatles: Get Back*', *Rock Music Studies* 9(2): 245–247.

Forbes, D., A. Korsgaard and H. Sapienza (2010) 'Financing decisions as a source of conflict in venture boards', *Journal of Business Venturing* 25: 579–592.

Foss, N. and P. G. Klein (2022) *Why Management Matters: The Perils of the Bossless Company* (New York: Public Affairs).

Francis, K. (2014) *The Making of John Lennon: The Untold Story of the Rise and Fall of the Beatles* (Edinburgh: Luath Press).

Ginting-Szczesny, B. A., E. Kibler, M. S. Cardon, T. Kautonen and H. Hakala (2023) 'The role of passion diversity, compassion, and self-compassion for team entrepreneurial passion', *Small Bus Economics*, https://doi.org/10.1007/s11187-023-00793-z.

Gould, J. (2007) *Can't Buy Me Love: The Beatles, Britain and America* (London: Piatkus).

Greathouse, J. (2015) 'This rookie mistake cost the Beatles $100,000,000', *Forbes*, 25 July, https://www.forbes.com/sites/johngreathouse/2015/07/25/this-rookie-mistake-cost-the-beatles-100000000/.

Harper, D. (2008) 'Towards a theory of entrepreneurial teams', *Journal of Business Venturing* 23: 613–626.

Haynes, J. and L. Marshall (2018) 'Reluctant entrepreneurs: musicians and entrepreneurship in the "new" music industry', *The British Journal of Sociology* 69(2): 459–482.

Hertsgaard, M. (1996) *A Day in the Life: The Music and Artistry of the Beatles* (London: Pan Books).

Huggins, R. and N. Williams (2009) 'Enterprise and public policy: a review of Labour government intervention in the United Kingdom', *Environment and Planning C: Government and Policy* 27(1): 19–41.

Jehn, K. A. (1995) 'A multimethod examination of the benefits and detriments of intragroup conflict', *Administrative Science Quarterly* 40(2): 256–282.

Jones, M. (2023) 'George Harrison at 80: the view from Liverpool' *Journal of Beatles Studies* 2(1): 159–163.

Jones, S. and W. Podrazik (2022) 'Streaming through a glass onion: Curation, chronology, control and the Beatles' legacy', *Journal of Beatles Studies* 1(1): 67–96.

Kapurch, K. and W. Everett (2020) '"If you become naked": sexual honesty on the Beatles' *White Album*', *Rock Music Studies* 7(3): 209–225.

Kapurch, K., M. Heyman and R. Mills (2023) *The Beatles and Humour: Mockers, Funny Paper and Other Play* (London: Bloomsbury).

Katzenbach, J. R. and D. K. Smith (2008) *The Discipline of Teams* (Brighton, MA: Harvard Business Press).

Khan, M. S., R. J. Breitenecker and E. J. Schwarz (2015) 'Adding fuel to the fire: Need for achievement diversity and relationship conflict in entrepreneurial teams', *Management Decision* 53(1): 75–99.

Klotz, A. C., K. M. Hmieleski, B. H. Bradley and L. W. Busentiz (2013) 'New venture teams: a review of the literature and roadmap for future research', *Journal of Management* 40(1): 226–255.

Langfred, C. W. (2007) 'The downside of self-management: a longitudinal study of the effects of conflict on trust, autonomy, and task interdependence in self-managing teams', *Academy of Management Journal* 50(4): 885–900.

Lazar, M., E. Miron-Spektor, R. Agarwal, M. Erez, B. Goldfarb and F. Chan (2020) 'Entrepreneurial team formation', *Academy of Management Annals* 14(1): 1–77.

Leick, B., S. Gretzinger and I. N. Roddvik (2023) 'Creative entrepreneurs and embeddedness in non-urban places: a resource exchange and network embeddedness logic', *International Journal of Entrepreneurial Behavior & Research* 29(5): 1133–1157.

Lewisohn, M. (1992) *The Complete Beatles Chronicle* (London: Harmony Books).

Lewisohn, M. (2013) *The Beatles – All These Years: Volume One: Tune In* (London: Little Brown).

MacDonald, I. (1994) *Revolution in the Head: The Beatles' Records and the Sixties* (London: Vintage).

McNab, K. (2015) *And in the End: The Last Days of the Beatles* (London: Polygon).

Miles, B. (1998) *Paul McCartney: Many Years from Now* (London: Owl Books).

Mohan, S. (2022) *Leadership Lessons with the Beatles: Actionable Tips and Tools for Becoming Better at Leading* (Abingdon: Routledge).

Nahapiet, J. and S. Ghoshal (1998) 'Social capital, intellectual capital, and the organizational advantage', *Academy of Management Review* 23(2): 242–266.

Norman, P. (2005) *Shout! The Beatles in their Generation* (London: Touchstone).

Patten, T. and S. Stephens (2023) 'The creative industries entrepreneur: an analysis of lived experience', *The Journal of Creative Behavior* 57(1): 49–64.

Patzelt, H., R. Preller and N. Breugst (2021) 'Understanding the life cycles of entrepreneurial teams and their ventures: an agenda for future research', *Entrepreneurship Theory and Practice* 45(5): 1119–1153.

Perry, R. (2009) *Northern Songs: The True Story of the Beatles Song Publishing Empire* (London: Music Sales).

Preller, R., N. Breugst and H. Patzelt (2016) 'Do we all see the same future? Entrepreneurial team members' visions and opportunity development', *Academy of Management Proceedings* 1: 13642.

Preller, R., H. Patzelt and N. Breugst (2020) 'Entrepreneurial visions in founding teams: conceptualization, emergence, and effects on opportunity development', *Journal of Business Venturing* 35(2): 105914.

Rachel, D. (2021) *Like Some Forgotten Dream: What if the Beatles Hadn't Split Up?* (London: Octopus).

Rosso, B. D. (2014) 'Creativity and constraints: exploring the role of constraints in the creative processes of research and development teams', *Organization Studies* 35(4): 551–585.

Schjoedt, L. and S. Kraus (2009) 'Entrepreneurial teams: definition and performance factors', *Management Research News* 32: 513–524.

Shane, S. and S. Venkataraman (2000) 'The promise of entrepreneurship as a field of research', *Academy of Management Review* 25(1): 217–226.

Slate, J. (2020) 'My transformative time with the Beatles in India', *The Daily Beast*, 6 September.

Spitz, B. (2005) *The Beatles: The Biography* (New York: Little, Brown).

Staley, S. R. (2020) *The Beatles and Economics* (Abingdon: Routledge).

Sunstein, C. (2022) 'Beatlemania: on informational cascades and spectacular success', *Journal of Beatles Studies* 1(1): 97–120.

Thompson, N. A. (2018) 'Imagination and creativity in organizations', *Organization Studies* 39(2/3): 229–250.

Tihula, S., J. Huovinen and M. Fink (2009) 'Entrepreneurial teams vs. managerial teams. Reasons for team formatting in small firms', *Management Research News* 32: 555–566.

Yin, J., M. Jia, Z. Ma and G. Liao (2020) 'Team leaders' conflict management styles and innovation performance in entrepreneurial teams', *International Journal of Conflict Management* 31(3): 373–392.

# Across the Universe

# Thinking with the Beatles
## On *Poppermost*

Andrew Wilson
wilsona2@tcd.ie

*For A. G. Cook*

Pacôme Thiellement's quite amazing book on the Beatles, *Poppermost: Considérations sur la mort de Paul McCartney* [Poppermost: Thoughts on the Death of Paul McCartney] was originally published in France in 2002.[1] It was reissued in 2013 with eight texts by an array of philosophers, writers, art historians, actors, directors and critics reflecting on the impact of the book both personally and on the French intellectual scene. In one of these appreciations the philosopher Mark Alizart writes, 'to re-read *Poppermost* today is to realize retroactively that the book was the dark precursor to one of the richest and most exciting moments in French intellectual life in recent memory [...] a moment that is perhaps still reverberating now'. Alizart goes on to say, 'if I had to characterize what *Poppermost* and an entire generation of Thiellementians like myself attempted to do with pop culture, I would have to say this: We were the first ones to take pop seriously'

---

1. 'Poppermost' is a neologism invented by John Lennon, a portmanteau word combining the popularness of pop with the dynamics of popping, making the whole into a superlative with the suffix -most.

(Thiellement 2013: 173–74).[2] Here, Alizart means something more than just taking pop seriously; he means taking it both seriously and affirmatively, even outrageously so.

For there have been any number of twentieth-century discourses (I'm thinking particularly of discourses on the left, where Thiellement also positions his work) that have arguably attempted to take mass culture seriously; it's just that these discourses didn't take it affirmatively. One could cite, for example, Clement Greenberg's 1939 essay 'Avant-garde and Kitsch', which appeared in the Marxist, though anti-Stalinist, *Partisan Review*; Theodor Adorno and Max Horkheimer's *The Dialectic of Enlightenment* of 1947, with its thoroughly gloomy chapter on what it calls the culture industry;[3] and finally, closer to home for Thiellement, Guy Debord's *Society of the Spectacle*, first published in France in 1967 and often seen as inspiration for the student protests of May '68. These three texts might even be thought of as forming something like the unspoken background to what Thiellement has to say in *Poppermost*, in as much as they can be seen as important strands in what we might call a prevailing twentieth-century discourse on the left (especially the Marxist left) when it comes to popular or mass culture.[4] Particular to all three of these strands is the belief that popular culture is now little more than a means for capitalism to extend its control from the workplace to what now only seemingly lies outside it: the domain of leisure. In this view, the first decades of the twentieth century witness an extension of the methods of rationalization and

---

2. All translations from the French, unless otherwise stated, are my own.
3. Adorno will be mentioned several times in what follows. This is owing not simply to his place in twentieth-century philosophy, but also to the fact that he was a classically trained composer himself, a student of Alban Berg, who consistently wrote on music (both high and low) throughout his career. Indeed, it would not be far off the mark to say that his work is at its heart an attempt to think twentieth-century music.
4. An obvious exception to this negative understanding of mass culture on the left would be British Cultural Studies. As Alizart points out, works by Stuart Hall and Raymond Williams were translated exceedingly late into French, 2007 for Hall and 2009 for Williams, both by the heterodox left press, Éditions Amsterdam, which was itself only founded in 2003.

organization of production (in principal mass production, standardization, the repetition of the same) to the new territory of art (by means of film, radio, photography, nascent television and the hit song). And while *Poppermost* is clearly at odds with this nothing if not reprobative, negative and gloomy assessment of popular culture coming from the left, it is important to see how Thiellement shares certain concerns and concepts with this tradition.

In other words, if Thiellement is implicitly writing against this tradition, he is writing against it as a kind of support, the way one writes against a table for example. Thus, it is important to my mind to see how Thiellement's affirmative line of thought is a kind of tangent that will repeatedly touch upon, cross paths with (i.e., sharing concerns and concepts) this other line of thought, all the while moving forward on its own, very different course.[5]

This is perhaps nowhere clearer than when it comes to the crucial distinction (within Marxism and elsewhere) between popular and mass culture. And even though Thiellement doesn't use the term mass culture (one can easily imagine why, considering the term's almost universal negative valence) and prefers his own near neologism pop,[6] I would argue that the concept is still ever present

---

5. There was also, of course, particularly in the pre- and immediate post-war period, an enthusiastic embrace of popular forms on the left (even using them for inspiration in high-art genres). We might think of the music of Aaron Copland, Walker Evans's photography and Orson Welles and John Houseman's Mercury Theatre (especially the experiments with radio of the Mercury Theatre on the Air) as particularly representative examples of this left populist persuasion. And indeed, these were, all three, favourite targets of Adorno and Horkheimer. Adorno was fond of saying that Copland's *Lincoln Portrait* could be found on the gramophone of every Stalinist intellectual (see *Minima Moralia*). For Adorno and Horkheimer, as well as for Debord, mass culture is a system whose aim is its own expansion, rather than any particular ideology. For example, Adorno and Horkheimer write that 'anyone who resists can only survive by being incorporated. Once registered as divergent by the culture industry, they belong to it as the land reformer does to capitalism. Realistic indignation is the trademark of those with a new idea to sell' (2002: 104). Debord, for his part, writes 'the spectacle aims at nothing other than itself' (1996: Thesis 14).
6. Thiellement's conception of pop is so particular to him, that is, so much wider than the typical meaning of the word, that I'm tempted to call it a neologism, although clearly it's not in the strict sense.

in *Poppermost*. For example, when Thiellement writes (in the chapter excerpted here) 'for a long time, "culture" was a weapon wielded by a people, that which adorned them with their most profound meaning, that which nourished their lives', he is referring precisely to a pre-industrial, pre-capitalist reality of culture that is no longer our own (except as particular survivals and pockets of underdevelopment) and that hasn't been for at least a century and a half. To my mind perhaps the clearest and best elaboration of this distinction is still found in Fredric Jameson's now classic essay (very much writing in the tradition of Adorno) 'Reification and Utopia in Mass Culture':

> The commercial products of mass culture can surely not without intellectual dishonesty be assimilated to so called popular, let alone folk, art of the past, which reflected and were dependent for their production on quite different social realities, and were in fact the 'organic' expression of so many distinct social communities or castes, such as the peasant village, the court, the medieval town, the polis, or even the classical bourgeoisie when it was still a unified social group with its own cultural specificity. The historically unique tendential effect of late capitalism on all such groups has been to dissolve and to fragment or atomize them into agglomerations (*Gesellschaften*) of isolated and equivalent private individuals, by way of the corrosive action of universal commodification and the market system. Thus, the 'popular' as such no longer exists, except under very specific and marginalized conditions (internal and external pockets of so called underdevelopment within the capitalist world system); the commodity production of contemporary or industrial mass culture has nothing whatsoever to do, and nothing in common, with older forms of popular or folk art. (Jameson 1992: 15)

Now, what is important to grasp about these older forms of popular or folk art is that they are tied not just to a particular people, to a particular community, but as well to a localizable place. Thus, there are Greek folk dances that are specific not just to the island of Crete but to particular villages on that island, and by looking closely at paintings by Pieter Bruegel the Elder you can learn a lot about the way pretzels were shaped differently depending on whether they were from this village or that in the sixteenth-century Dutch countryside. These popular forms are expressions of an identity, of a *lebenswelt*, a particular lifeworld. Joseph Leo Koerner in his quite amazing book on Hieronymus Bosch and Bruegel nicely describes this localizable aspect of popular forms when discussing Bruegel's *The Peasant Dance*:

> The pots displayed in *The Peasant Dance* are stylistically homogenous. They form what an ethnographic museum might gather and exhibit as the assemblage of a particular culture. Different from pots made in a village around the bend, they are nonetheless timeless: things made here rather than elsewhere, but always in the same way. The actions in Bruegel's painting would belong to this assemblage. If somehow we could hear the melodies, feel the rhythms, and catch the patterns of the dance, we would grasp the local color of these revels, as specific as the beaded bases of the pots, as unique as the bit of the housewife's iron key. (Koerner 2016: 273)

I don't want to leave the impression that this distinction between older popular or folk cultures and modern post-industrialization culture is only to be found within Marxism — it isn't. For example, Koerner's influences are phenomenological/Heideggerian, which is also a touchstone for Thiellement. And I might add that the subject matter of Bruegel's painting, that is, music and dance, is in no way beside the point for our current discussion of the Beatles. And I would suggest that it is precisely this kind of distinction between culture as a lifeworld of a particular community and pop as it manifests itself post-industrialization that informs virtually everything Thiellement has to say about the Beatles. For example, when he writes that 'America, or more precisely African Americans, invented the blues, jazz, rock: "primitive, authentic music"', he means primitive and authentic not as insults but rather as descriptors pertaining to lifeworlds. (Thus, primitive for Thiellement should in no way be confused with Adorno and Horkheimer's describing jazz as 'aesthetic barbarism'.)[7]

---

7. Adorno and Horkheimer's pronouncements on jazz are to be found in an early essay from 1936 by Adorno entitled 'On jazz', and in *The Dialectic of Enlightenment*. It's worth mentioning that 'jazz' for them refers to what would more precisely be called swing, which it's fair to say had conquered Weimar Germany. Even Adorno's

The important point here is to see how American blues at its origins is the authentic expression of the lifeworld of African Americans living in the Mississippi Delta. It is generally accepted that blues music was first recorded in June 1926, though it is thought to have existed at least since the turn of the twentieth century (Gioia 2009). The question then becomes whether it is really helpful to use the same descriptors when talking about music written by two young Teddy Boys who recognize each other's style while riding on a bus in Liverpool and strike up a conversation, which then leads to them visiting each other at home where they will play for each other their favourite records, among which are American blues compilations.[8] Or, rather, whether some line has been irremediably crossed.

Now, it would be easy to say that this line that has been crossed is recorded music or the record. However, I think things are a good bit more complicated than that, especially for Thiellement. We might say that the record condenses at least three streams (technological, economic and artistic) and that these three streams form a whole that is difficult to pry apart, where each individual stream acts upon the other two, creating what we might call a complex manifold. Thus, the record commodifies music in a new and more intensive way, connecting music to industry, what one quite readily calls now, without a second thought, the music industry. And here it's important to see that for Thiellement there is no understanding of the Beatles that does not pass through an understanding of the commodity. This is no less true for Thiellement than it is for Adorno and Horkheimer when they confront jazz. And it is Thiellement's attention to music as a commodity that will lead to his

---

most sympathetic readers now basically admit that his opinions on jazz were ill-informed and misguided. Gerhard Schweppenhäuser (2009: 111–12, 149), for example, sees the 1936 essay 'On jazz' as doing little more than offering justification for the various attempts of the Nazi party to prohibit jazz which had begun as early as 1933 with the formation of the Reichsmusikkammer (the German Ministry of Music).

8. I suspect that there is more than one account of Lennon and McCartney's first meeting, but here I have extrapolated from McCartney's own telling in an interview with Sean Lennon from 2020, https://www.youtube.com/watch?v=iCe8fdBeTCs (accessed 19 April 2024).

quite startling (one might say heretical, from both a Marxist and a psychoanalytic standpoint) rethinking of both commodity fetishism and fandom. The chapter of *Poppermost* excerpted here offers nothing less than a positive theory of commodity fetishism, as well as an understanding of fandom as a kind of knowledge. I'll leave it to the reader to discover these arguments in Thiellement's inimitable prose. The one thing I would point out, however, is the way that these arguments think not simply the impact of commodification on music, but as well the impact of music on commodification, or more specifically here, consumption.[9] Is not Beatlemania the word we have for a new kind of consumption that cannot simply be thought economically, but must also be thought musically and libidinally? Even today, watching clips of the 1964 Shea Stadium concert on YouTube would seem to make this thought unavoidable.

The effects of the record, and by extension recording, on music, however, do not end there. The record is a kind of deterritorialization of music, loosening its ties to a particular time and space. And here we reach Thiellement's most ambitious, and perhaps most difficult to grasp, concepts: originary expropriation and the enigmatic, and hard to translate, figure of the *tour*. In some sense, the French word *tour* is for Thiellement a privileged figure of originary expropriation, since it combines in one word at least three meanings: a turn in either space or time (a turn of events), thus a figure of change; a turning that returns to its point of departure (like a revolution of a record, *un tour de disque* in French), thus a figure of repetition; and finally the sense of a trick, a card trick (*un tour de cartes*) or magic trick (*un tour de magie*), suggesting a sleight of hand or detour that produces a spellbinding effect. That these three senses do not exist together in one English word only makes it all the more remarkable that the Beatles seem to have successfully (and economically) rendered them with the

---

9. It's important to see here that Thiellement's treatment of fandom is not quantitative but rather qualitative. His interest is not in record sales, chart positions, but rather the intensities of the fan experience. This is just one of the ways that *Poppermost* differs from what we could call a populist understanding of popular forms.

phrase magical mystery tour. Thiellement will go on to find facets of the *tour* throughout the Beatles, from the notion of revolver to the nurse in 'Penny Lane' who sells poppies (the flower of pop for Thiellement) in the middle of the roundabout, by way, of course, of 'Revolution #9'. As a figure of both repetition and change, what we might call a repetition of difference, the word *tour* points towards an understanding of mass production as not simply the repetition of the same.[10]

Whatever else they might be, originary expropriation and the figure of the *tour* are Thiellement's way to think the transition from popular to mass culture affirmatively, that is, no longer through the logics of loss and castration (notice that this is precisely what Thiellement does with the psychoanalytic concept of fetishism when he declares, for example, that 'the fetishist isn't unhappy'. To put the argument rather bluntly, yes, the record is a substitute for the live performance, but we shouldn't then leap to the conclusion that the live performance was Mummy's phallus which is now missing.)[11] So yes, the record is a deterritorialization that detaches music from a particular time and place, and at least potentially supplants the concert as the most developed form of the composition.[12] This is the lesson Thiellement will draw from the Beatles' *Sgt. Pepper's Lonely*

---

10. The philosophical background to these ideas would certainly include Gilles Deleuze's *Difference and Repetition* (Deleuze 1994). In *Poppermost*, the word *tour* (in its various forms) is nothing if not resonant. Often, it is meant to resonate with Nietzsche's eternal return, but at other moments the resonances can be farther afield, or even far-fetched, that is, possibly just imagined by the reader. For instance, how might Thiellement's *tour* interpellate the ancient Greek πολύτροπος (literally, 'turning many ways'), which is the first adjective applied to Odysseus in *The Odyssey*?

11. Admittedly, this is a scandalously abbreviated version of ideas laid out over the two volumes of French philosopher Gilles Deleuze and psychoanalyst Félix Guattari's work *Capitalism and Schizophrenia*.

12. For a parallel understanding of recorded music that is admirably attuned to the ontological stakes of the record, see Paul Long's 'The poetics of recorded time: listening again to popular music history' (2019). Long's reading of the place of the phonograph record in Sartre's *Nausea* suggests that that 1938 novel is very much part of the conversation between philosophy and twentieth-century music that I am trying to unpack here.

*Hearts Club Band*. Here, he quotes George Martin to great effect: 'They were songs that you couldn't play in concert. Songs written to be listened to on a record. That's what's important' (Martin 1995, qtd in Thiellement 2013: 47). One could draw a line from Paul Hindemith and Ernst Toch's *Neue Musik Berlin* of 1930,[13] an experiment in 'made-for-phonograph-record music' (*Originalschallplattenmusik*) with its superimposition of various phonograph recordings and live musical performances, which employed variations in speed, pitch and acoustic timbre, to Karlheinz Stockhausen's *Kontakte* of 1960 with its use of tape loops (the same Stockhausen who appears on the cover of *Sgt. Pepper* and figured on John and Yoko's Christmas card list in the 1960s), to the tape loop experiments on 'Tomorrow Never Knows' in 1966 and on *Sgt. Pepper* the year after, to Auto-Tune and P.C. Music now.[14] And what this line describes is the various ways in which recording is not simply something that happens to music (from the outside, as it were), but that music is also something that happens to recording.

And yet here we reach a further twist (*tour*) in Thiellement's argument. We said earlier that the record condenses at least

---

13. It is not insignificant that Adorno disallowed the possibility of phonograph-specific music like that of Hindemith and Toch in an essay published in *Musikblätter des Ansbruch*, four years after *Neue Musik Berlin*. The most relevant sentence reads: 'Just as the call for "radio-specific" music remained necessarily empty and unfulfilled and gave rise to nothing better than some directions for instrumentation that turned out to be impracticable, so too there has never been any gramophone-specific music' (Adorno 1990: 56—57). I am indebted to Thomas Y. Levin's 'For the record: Adorno on music in the age of its technological reproducibility' for my thinking about *Neue Musik Berlin* in particular and about the record more generally.

14. I would never say that this is a straight line, but it's a line all the same. The best place to go for a primer on the thought, if not the music, of the London electronic music collective and record label P.C. Music is the short film entitled *The Art of the Muses*, which appears at time stamp 1:42:35 in the live stream entitled *Away From Keyboard [file not found]*, https://www.youtube.com/watch?v=Qohp5raSFYQ (accessed 19 April 2024). I hesitate to bring up the highly disputed term hyperpop for this type of music, but I'll mention it only because it does offer a near perfect interpellation of John Lennon's portmanteau word, poppermost. On John and Yoko's Christmas card list and other connections between the Beatles and the Darmstadt avant-garde, see Ross (2007).

three streams (technological, economic and artistic). Now we must add a fourth, ontological, stream; for this, it seems to me, is what originary expropriation is. If you pay close attention to the letter of Thiellement's text, you will notice his use of the word *revelation* (pop is the revelation of *originary expropriation*), or even the word *annunciation*, meaning for him 'the anticipatory formulation of a kind of revelation'. What I take this to mean is that pop, which includes the record, and by extension recording, does not cause originary expropriation, it is rather the revealing, the announcement, of something that is, in its essence, ontological. (Put another way, Thiellement's discourse is far from a technological determinism.) And what Thiellement forces you to think is precisely an ontology that is, in its very essence, improper, that is, in some sense, not what it is — not just a concatenation of accidents and essences, but something much weirder where accident and essence are something like the same thing. So, pop is cultural through and through, and *Poppermost* can be read as a cultural history of popular music in the West in the post-war period, a strange history to be sure, but a cultural history all the same — thus, a culture that in some sense can be placed and dated, however vaguely, notwithstanding its deterritorializations. But this reading as cultural history is doubled by another reading, like a mirror image of the first or, better yet, a tape loop now played backwards. And in this reading what was, just a moment ago, cultural is now ontological and points to something that is almost immemorial, originary expropriation. Everything has changed, and yet nothing has changed.

So, the concept of originary expropriation is the ontology of a culture that is, in its essence, improper, that is, *a culture made from odds and ends, a kind of bric-a-brac of contradictory influences, of references consumed on the run* as Thiellement says, and while this concept will inform virtually all the distinctions Thiellement lays out (that between popular culture and mass culture, or what he just calls pop; that between blues, jazz, early rock at their origins and the Beatles; that between America and England; that between pop as represented by what for him are its six great geniuses, the Beatles, David Bowie and Brian Eno, and rock, now not in its 'primitive', authentic African-American form, but rock as a mere pose that still pretends to authenticity and primitiveness and as represented by its own string of great geniuses from Elvis Presley to Kurt Cobain, by way of Jim Morrison, Lou Reed and Iggy Pop), it is important to see that the concept is itself improper. Originary expropriation is itself, as a concept, *made from odds and ends, a kind of bric-a-brac of contradictory influences, of references consumed on the run*, a kind of *tour de cartes*, a kind of sleight of hand magic trick. For how could it be otherwise? Either the culture is, in its essence (i.e., ontologically, including the very concept of its improperness) improper or it isn't. To claim some sort of properness for one's own concept of the improper is a move that is beneath a thinker of Thiellement's calibre. This is what Thiellement quite explicitly says in an important, italicized passage (a kind of meta-commentary on the book itself) later in *Poppermost*:

> Here we clearly see the problem posed by a book like this: It can only be fictional, since it adopts the contents of fiction. And in as much as it is theoretical, it is such only through an inevitable formal effect that has to do with its treatment of what it has to say. In its deepest depths, it must admit that it is novelistic. If it doesn't, its discourse will quickly become unbearable, and many questions will remain unanswered. For example, questions like this one: How do you talk about metaphysical truth when you don't believe in it? (Thiellement 2013: 63—64)

If I might be allowed to venture an answer to Thiellement's question above, what you do is look for a new metaphysics. And I would say that is what originary expropriation is.

Admittedly, this improperness of the very concept of originary expropriation can make *Poppermost* difficult to follow. Thiellement's line of thought is continually circling back to what it said a moment ago, not in order to restate but rather to unsettle what was just said. This circling back is itself the figure of the *tour*, both circle and trick. In the chapter excerpted here, we encounter this most clearly when Thiellement returns to the idea of primitiveness via the nineteenth-century French poet Charles Baudelaire. Just a moment ago, primitiveness was the foundation upon which any number of distinctions were being built, and pop was precisely 'the putting in quotation marks of all primitivism', but now, suddenly, through a passage from Baudelaire's journal from exile in Belgium, the primitive becomes another version, another avatar, of pop. To quote Baudelaire's reverie on the native peoples of North America:

> His clothes, his finery, his weapons, his ceremonial objects, all bear witness to an inventiveness which has long since forsaken us. Dandyism is the last glimmer of heroism in its final decadent stage. And the type of dandy the traveler encounters in North America in no way discourages this thought, since nothing stops us from supposing that the tribes we describe as savage are in fact the remains of great civilizations, now disappeared. (Thiellement 2013: 43)

And now, just like that, primitivism is swept up into the movement of originary expropriation and reinscribed as a form of dandyism, and Thiellement will waste no time reminding us who the great twentieth-century dandies are: Paul McCartney, Brian Jones, the Who, the Kinks, David Bowie, Robert Smith...

## Bibliography

Adorno, Theodor (1990) 'On jazz', trans. Jamie Owen Daniel, *Discourse* 12, *A Special Issue on Music*: 45–69.
Adorno, Theodor (1995) 'The form of the phonograph record', trans. Thomas Y. Levin, *October* 5: 56–61.
Adorno, Theodor and Max Horkheimer (2002) *The Dialectic of Enlightenment*, trans. Edmund Jephcott (Palo Alto, CA: Stanford University Press).
Debord, Guy (1996) *La Société du spectacle* (Paris: Gallimard).
Deleuze, Gilles (1994) *Difference and Repetition*, trans. Paul Patton (New York: Columbia University Press).
Deleuze, Gilles and Félix Guattari (1983) *Anti-Oedipus: Capitalism and Schizophrenia*, vol. 1, trans. Robert Hurley, Mark Seem and Helen R. Lane (Minneapolis: University of Minnesota Press).
Deleuze, Gilles and Félix Guattari (1987) *A Thousand Plateaus: Capitalism and Schizophrenia*, vol. 2, trans. Brian Massumi (Minneapolis: University of Minnesota Press).

Gioia, Ted (2009) *Delta Blues: The Life and Times of the Mississippi Masters Who Revolutionized American Music* (New York: W.W. Norton).
Jameson, Fredric (1992) 'Utopia and reification in mass culture', in *Signatures of the Visible* (London: Routledge), 9–34.
Koerner, Joseph Leo (2016) *Bosch & Bruegel, From Enemy Painting to Everyday Life* (Princeton, NJ: Princeton University Press).
Levin, Thomas Y. (1990) 'For the record: Adorno on music in the age of its technological reproducibility', *October* 55: 23–47.
Long, Paul (2019) 'The poetics of recorded time: listening again to popular music history', *Popular Music History* 12(3): 295–315.
Martin, George with William Pearson (1995) *With a Little Help From My Friends: The Making of Sgt. Pepper* (Boston: Little, Brown).
Ross, Alex (2007) *The Rest is Noise: Listening to the Twentieth Century* (New York: Farrar, Straus and Giroux).
Schweppenhäuser, Gerhard (2009) *Theodor W. Adorno: An Introduction*, trans. James Rolleston (Durham, NC: Duke University Press).
Thiellement, Pacôme (2013) *Poppermost: Considérations sur la mort de Paul McCartney*, 2nd edn (Paris: Éditions MF).

# Poppermost

Pacôme Thiellement

Translated from the French by Andrew Wilson
wilsona2@tcd.ie

> Enjoying a crowd is an art given only to those who binge on vitality at the expense of their humanity, only to those whom a fairy visited in their cradle, instilling in them a taste for transvestism and the mask, a hatred of home and a love of travel.
>
> Charles Baudelaire

Many books have offered detailed explanations of Beatles songs. In them, for instance, you might learn that 'Lucy in the Sky with Diamonds' is a drawing by John Lennon's son or that 'Being for the Benefit of Mr. Kite' was inspired by an old poster possessed by one of the bandmates, again John Lennon. But that is not in the least the purpose here. Our object is specifically the elucidation of what one means by pop culture and how that culture might be, and in fact *is*, an event in human history. Logically enough, this elucidation will entail a meditation on the source of pop culture, which is none other than pop music, as well as on the relations pop music maintains with thought and poetry. What's more, pop is an event of such magnitude that its emergence in a certain way carries within it the possibility for humans like us to re-evaluate what we mean by humanity, by culture, by world and society.

In what follows, we will suggest that the emergence of something like pop music was a necessity, and the same goes for the pop culture that followed, but that these two events in art history, as well as in the history of thought (since what we are proposing is no less than a pop philosophy, and we owe that very term to none other than Gilles Deleuze and Félix Guattari) have yet to be brought into relation with the period in which we're living. Indeed, pop music and the pop culture that stems from it gives us the truth of that period, far more than some work coming out of an academic discipline. This is not news: the university is exhausted. The social sciences are exhausted, philosophy too. But that does not mean that we will subscribe here to the voluntary theoretical negligence of the rock critic — far from it.

One of the principal problems posed at the outset of this work is how does one re-evaluate the status of pop culture, by which we mean popular culture, when the very term popular culture is itself problematic. Pop culture only has meaning in so far as it is already situated inside the pre-defined field of culture. But 'culture' itself in our contemporary sense is a recent idea. For a long time, 'culture' was a weapon wielded by a people, that which adorned them with their most profound meaning, that which nourished their lives. 'Culture' today, however, is merely the receptacle into which we pour works (of various significance) that are both by and for people of a certain milieu or social class. Thus, working-class culture, elitist culture, French culture or American culture. Also, of a certain tendency: right-wing culture or leftist culture.

Rock, like the blues, country or jazz, first appeared as a popular culture. Popular is here meant in several different senses: First of all, it refers to the origins of its representatives (if we think of Robert Johnson, Hank Williams, Elvis Presley or Louis Armstrong), after that to the 'milieu' of its principal audience, and finally popular because it achieved popular success. To say 'a song is popular' means that it is both recognized and appreciated by a vast number of people. In this regard, the primacy given to melody is hardly beside the point.

One typically dates the distinction between true culture, today high culture, and popular or pop culture, its poor cousin — today having become in our (post-pro-situationist) verbiage, the spectacle — to the onset of industrialization. But since culture has, in any number of instances, been an ideological support for either those in power or those fighting against them, this separation of true culture and popular culture essentially comes down to a distinction between the consumers of these cultures. Upper-class consumers are destined to consume pseudo-true (high) culture while the lower classes, given their more modest education, settle for the pseudo-popular (pop) culture. This separation however, while both economic and social, tells us nothing about the kind of thought that appears in the works one deems — often after a brief interregnum in the midst of the avant-garde — as 'artistic' or 'popular'. And the same goes for the interpreters of these cultures, with their 'specialists' writing for a necessarily limited audience, typically characterized as the well-off, having had a lengthy apprenticeship in school, or, on the other hand, the 'vulgarizers' speaking to the public at large. But no one says anything about the thought contained within — about that, we know nothing, since it's simply a difference of class, of social milieu. No real qualitative distinction separates the two cultures.

The ambiguity only becomes more present when difficult intellectual or artistic figures, after a period in the domain of 'elitist culture', pass into the common trove as representatives of a particular period or civilization: Freud, Marx, Picasso, Mozart, Rimbaud, for instance. Or equally when artistic or cultural figures thought of as 'popular' are suddenly seen as possessing other facets, as in some sense 'misunderstood', which in turn leads to serious study by specialists. Thus, Chaplin, Hitchcock, Duke Ellington, Groucho Marx, Molière and Shakespeare, for example. Here, we are oddly at a loss when it comes to the pertinent criteria for assigning works their 'cultural' or 'artistic' significance. The demarcation between true and popular culture is instead to be found in the very essence of the modern world, which transforms all thought, all expression, into *culture*, that is, into an unconditioned production, instantly available for consumption, and as a result divided into sectors in order to facilitate assimilation. Thus, the reinterpretation of virtually every achievement of human history as so much culture is for Heidegger one of the five essential phenomena of modernity (alongside science, mechanized technology, the placing of art within the horizon of aesthetics, and the loss of the gods). 'It belongs to the essence of civilization as culture to cultivate itself in turn, and thus to become a politics of culture' ('The Age of the World Picture').

In other words, popular culture, pop culture, is nothing in itself: it is only the desired depository for all the materials which are immediately consumable. The relative difference in importance stems only from an interpretation, or from the milieu that provides the interpretation, more precisely, from the milieu which is allowed to give it. And it should be noted that, alas, this interpretation is little more than an *a priori* judgement. No thinker working since the 1950s has seriously tried to think the field of pop culture on its own terms, in other words to treat the work of Chuck Berry, Roy Orbison, Jimi Hendrix, Robert Crumb... as a meaningful discourse, without immediately saddling it with a host of sociological, linguistic or psychoanalytic terms, which reduce considerably the meaning and lead, almost without fail, to texts saturated with the subjectivity of their authors, and often motivated by their own personal conflicts.

It's clear: What we now call culture unites no one. Today, the status of what in the past went by that name is now closer to a form of oppression, a generator of stress and social separation. Moreover, we've grown used to this: that culture is incapable of appearing as a whole, and yet it still manages to exercise a coercive power over the entire community, making its members feel guilty, with characteristics more akin to the religions which are otherwise on the decline, and all this generates little more than the guilty conscience of the last man — having killed god all together, we now insist on blaming each other.

The decline of that culture that one thinks of as 'Western' is in large part due to the reduction of the distances separating the different parts of the globe. A reduction of distance first for the naive missionaries who thought that the other cultures had to be gathered together, reunited, and thus surpassed in a kind of revelation: reunited inside the Universal, that is, the Western model, which refers to no one in particular, and yet jealously vampirizes all the energies, establishing a kind of non-place from which everything can be separated out and corrected. And next, for our more subtle thinkers, for whom the encounter with other cultures would amount to the revelation of their radical alterity. Gone forever would be the idea of a universality upon which one could base the principles of a single global culture or of a single global politics. *But then why in hell should the other be any more real, any more radical, any more authentic than ourselves?* Quickly enough, however, the idea of a regionalized multiculturalism was itself destined to fail, since the reduction of distances led indeed to a kind of cultural cross-fertilization, but this, far from progressively creating one people which could then be administered by one law, one juridical system, one faculty of judgement, instead simply accentuated the gaps, rendering any imagined assimilation impossible, the singularities having become more and more insular, more and more irreducible.

It's James Joyce's response to Nazism to have written *Finnegans Wake* in a carefully constructed mutant language, foreign to itself, in order to drive to despair anyone wishing to fall back on *one* language, *one* culture that might pretend to be an origin, and thus in that way establish a universal truth. Joyce's statement, when word came of the invasion of Poland, that the Germans would've been better off reading *Finnegans Wake* has rarely been taken seriously. And yet there Joyce's entire mythical machinery is put in the service of a multitude of singularities, extracted from History one by one, and sent into a strange aleatory vortex, towards the riskiest of destinations. *Finnegans Wake* was an annunciation, the anticipatory formulation of a kind of revelation: The revelation of *originary expropriation*, of errancy, of the absence of any propriety upon which to base our existence. No, the reign of the gods will never return, not because it is now past, but rather because it never existed as we thought. It was never anything other than a luminous chaos, a kind of innocence in which we are forever caught, whether we like it or not. Let us repeat: we are *simulacra*. We are playthings. And it is only when we begin to see just how much we are playthings that we begin to be free, that is, that we begin to play this game called Existence all the way to the end ('Play the game Existence to the end of the beginning', 'Tomorrow Never Knows', *Revolver*, 1966), an end that is none other than the veritable beginning. From now on, we must stop thinking of 'the' culture in order to think instead in terms of a mutant cultivation, heterogeneous, composite, improper, but once again innocent and animal, singular and joyous, in short: *pop*. And pop culture is nothing other than a means of cultivation that draws its poetical sources from pop music.

Pop music is a popular music that, unlike blues, country, jazz or rock, appropriates the styles of other kinds of music, without any predetermined rule, as though by chance, and yet with each song it finds itself forced to invent new (rhythmic, melodic) rules, which sometimes last only for the length of one song. Thus, pop music radically brings into question the very possibility of the proper, of origin, of authenticity, each time proposing nothing but artifice, the improper, junk, a small wonder, a becoming, an enchantment, in short: a sacred experience. To make the chaos lurking inside us 'a star that dances' (Nietzsche).

America, or more precisely African Americans, invented the blues, jazz, rock: 'primitive', authentic music. England's response was to invent pop, which is the bringing into doubt of any originary authenticity, the putting into quotation marks of all primitivism, a clean break inside the chaos of a dancing star. And ever since, all music, be it European or American (or, rather, African-American), has been in one form or another a response to pop. Sampling is a pop invention, rap is a pop invention, techno is a pop invention, acid house is a pop invention, industrial music is a pop invention, since each one is improper, retroactive, a music of mixes and remixes.

Pop is the revelation of *originary expropriation*. Pop culture is a culture made from odds and ends, a kind of bric-a-brac of contradictory influences, of references consumed on the run, a dense and implosive mix of trash culture. Pop culture is also, and above all, the consummate and acknowledged culture of the fragment. Of course, all modern works of art are fragmentary, but it is left to pop to make the fragment fun, a pleasure, even a joy, pure bliss, and not simply a kind of mourning for something lacking at the heart of being. Pop is any culture that wholeheartedly assumes its fragmentary character as a necessity and not as some kind of accident that has befallen it from the outside. Culture has always been fragmentary, but it has never dared to think itself as such, or at least not since ancient Greece in the West and India in the East. And for good reason: Culture has always believed in an authentic source, in a model which engenders its history, and not in a procession of simulacra pushing the work towards a systematic and natural fragmentation.

In *Capital*, Marx writes the following as a kind of remembrance of the London Universal Exposition of 1851:

> It's apparent that human activity transforms the material provided by nature in such a way as to make it useful. If one makes a table, for example, the shape of the wood is changed. Nonetheless, the table is still wood, an ordinary thing that is still available to the senses... But as soon as it appears as a commodity, the situation is entirely changed. At once graspable and ungraspable, it is now not enough for the table as commodity to rest its legs on the ground, it stands, so to speak, on its wooden head before the other commodities and indulges in fancies stranger than if it began to dance.

(Moreover, there is an actual dancing table in a George Harrison music video.) But within pop culture, dancing becomes the ultimate expression of wisdom: that joyous, daring, intense, fresh Nietzschean wisdom. 'As a being of lightness, Zarathustra recalled, how could I possibly be an enemy of the divine dance? Or of the graceful feet of young girls?' In this sense, pop culture is a very British invention, or rather, an invention of the most British of French poets, Charles Baudelaire. As Giorgio Agamben writes:

> At the beginning of the Second Industrial Revolution, Baudelaire drew from the transfiguration of the commodity during the Paris Universal Exposition of 1855 the emotional atmosphere and symbolic elements of his poetics. The great novelty that the Exposition had made obvious to Baudelaire's perceptive eye was that the commodity had ceased to be an innocent object... And once the commodity had freed objects of use from the slavery of being useful, the borderline that separated them from works of art — the borderline that artists from the Renaissance forward had indefatigably worked to establish by basing it on the supremacy of artistic creation over the mere 'making' of the artisan and the laborer — could only become extremely tenuous... The greatness of Baudelaire with respect to the invasion of the commodity

was that he responded to this invasion by transforming the work of art into a commodity and fetish... But what gives his discovery a genuinely revolutionary character is that Baudelaire did not limit himself to reproducing within the artwork the scission between use-value and exchange value, but also proposed to create a commodity in which the form of value would be totally identified with the use-value: an *absolute* commodity, so to speak, in which the process of fetishization would be pushed to the point of annihilating the reality of the commodity itself as such... The absolute commodification of the work of art is also *the most radical abolition of the commodity*. (*Stanzas: Word and Phantasm in Western Culture*)

Moreover, the pop consumer is almost always a fetishist, bordering on obsessional and compulsive behaviour. You can see it in his immoderate love of merchandising, which the Beatles were the first to engage in: hats, mugs, tee-shirts, glasses, pins, lighters... 'The fetishist', writes Baudrillard, 'pulls off that miracle of erasing the accidental nature of the world, substituting for it an absolute necessity.' The pop consumer desires a lock of the pop star's hair; if he manages to touch him, he promises to never wash his hand. The pop consumer makes things sacred: He must ritualize everything he loves, creating for himself magical objects, blessing everything he touches with his cosmic eros. 'I defy any art lover to love a painting as much as a fetishist loves a shoe', wrote Georges Bataille, quite to the point. We could just as well speak of a 12-year-old fan of the Spice Girls. Any artist who doesn't see that the real challenge lies here, in other words who isn't concerned by his inability to move others, to make them tremble and shake, vibrate and convulse in almost painful ecstasies, but rather is content to offer his intellectual precedence and plastic achievements, or even worse, an authentic experience — such an artist is a pig who deserves to perish in the mud of his artistic respectability. 'What is art?', asks Baudelaire, before immediately responding: 'Prostitution.' Freud defines fetishism as the horrified sight of the mother's missing phallus, which then leads the fetishist to focus on a compensatory object. In this regard, Freud remains inside the guilty conscience of the last man: There is no god, there is nothing which is proper, but we carry inside us the mark of this absence, with sadness and distress. We construct our unconscious on the basis of a consciousness of this lack, on the guilty conscience of our originary expropriation. But it isn't the case, and Freud has gone massively astray: The fetishist isn't unhappy, and he's no sicker than you or me. He sanctifies what he desires (a shoe, a Spice Girls record) with a gesture both erotic and sacred. In this way, he reconnects with the condition of primitive man. Because primitive man never believed in some model that had subsequently escaped his consciousness. He never thought in terms of a supposed authenticity that he had one day lost. The primitive makes himself up, paints his face, arrays himself in ample jewellery, with magical amulets and painted weapons. The primitive is, properly speaking, he who couldn't care less about the proper, he who *the absence of the proper is itself a kind of propriety,* he who doesn't see the difference between nature and culture, for whom artifice is an integral part of the real, contained in the real as much as the real is contained in artifice. In other words, primitive man is an English gentleman. Nothing could be further from primitive man than some sort of naturalism. Far be it from him to look for authenticity in his relations with nature. It's again Baudelaire who will be the first to focus on primitive man, not in order to exalt his goodness in the state of nature (that classic Rousseauism), but rather his elegance, his imagination as the bearer of an extremely refined immemorial culture. 'His clothes, his finery, his weapons, his ceremonial objects, all bear witness to an inventiveness which has long since forsaken us.' Thus, the nomad of shamanistic societies becomes the most obvious predecessor to the dandy. 'Dandyism is the last glimmer of heroism in its final decadent stage: And the type of dandy the traveler encounters in North America in no way discourages this thought, since nothing stops us from supposing that the tribes we describe as savage are in fact the remains of great civilizations, now disappeared.' In as much as it seriously engages with fetishism and tends towards immediate incarnations of the dandy (Paul McCartney, Brian Jones, the Who, the Kinks, David Bowie, Robert Smith...), pop culture has about it, as its immediate effect, a certain kind of new primitivism, in the words of Scott Batty, a chic primitivism. In this sense, it takes into account and supports the most difficult of thoughts: That there are no proper entities, and there never have been (we are always already thrown into expropriation), that the most serious work of art is that which adorns itself in the shimmering colours of the primitive, and yet it must maintain the frosty bearing of the dandy, all the while provoking the hyper-erotic excitement of the fetish — in other words, it must create a fanaticism close to that experienced for pop stars, and this: in order to exist as a necessity.

The earth is 'that which is light' (Zarathustra), because it is the expropriated *par excellence*; it is errant, that which turns (*la tournante*). And in our turn, our trick (*notre tour*) must be in the image of the earth. Any halting in the cycle of metamorphoses, any basis one might wish to undergird or project beyond the simple 'dancing star', is now little more than error and alienation. But truth is not so much opposed to error as it is to the supposed permanence we insist on seeing as truth. Truth is errancy, while permanence is alienation. And any thought that thinks errancy in relation to a lost or lacking permanence is not just false but mediocre, for it is just the unhappy thought of the last man, that of the most hideous of men. There isn't, nor has there ever been, an object in itself, all that exists are sacred practices traversing objects. There are no objects as such, and the unique work of art is in fact neither unique nor autonomous: it lives by traversing lives with its originary expropriation, and in fact has never been anything other than that *absolute commodity that abolishes all commodities by instituting a sacred presence.*

The inauguration of pop culture doesn't merely stand between the classical period and our post-industrial present, it turns great works of the past into pop: Mozart and Satie are now pop. Baudelaire and Wilde are pop. But not everything is pop (St Thomas Aquinas and Kant will have a hard time passing themselves off as such), rather only those works of art of the past that manage to rival a Madonna or Michael Jackson record in seduction and fascination, all the while offering something else, the infinite richness of interpretation, complexity of sensation and depth of exploration that one associates with great works of art. The rest, no, for they continue to proclaim their authenticity, their sad cultural apartness in the face of the fascination exerted by American action films and Japanese video games. 'Therefore, poets, try to outdo the labels on perfume bottles' (Guillaume Apollinaire, 'The Musician of Saint-Merry').

*

Paul McCartney: 'The Americans had a very particular way of doing things. The American Dream perhaps. On the *Ed Sullivan Show*, they used to have jugglers, magicians, entertainers, and that's what Frank Sinatra, Frank Jr, even Elvis still were. But the Beatles had this other approach: to take all the various nuances, and make them British, and then our particular chemistry did the rest. We worked a lot on this British way of doing things and it didn't come right away. Everything we imagined eventually fell into place. But we were lucky and it took longer than we thought.' Pop music is both a British and a Baudelairean invention; it is England's response to America (America, the land that brought us Pop Art, which is fundamentally different from pop culture in that it tries to arrest our understanding of the phenomenon, by anchoring it to art history and thus dating it).

Baudelaire's absolute commodity was a response to the Paris Universal Exposition of 1855; pop music is a response to the Marshall Plan. 'America bombards us with vapid, indifferent things, with simulacra of life...', complained Rainer Maria Rilke. When, in the wake of something as all-encompassing as the Marshall Plan, Europe had to make do with the vapid and the indifferent, whether it liked it or not, England, instead of complaining, responded by filling these simulacra with odds and ends, odds and ends which evoked the entire weight of European history, turning that chaos into something light, a star that dances. When offered the weighty void of authenticity, it chose instead a seductive lightness, full of artifice: *the force of the amulet* (Baudelaire). The Baroque had returned in democratic form, as well as *that superiority of nomadic peoples, of sheepherders and hunter gatherers, even of cannibals* (again, Baudelaire), over the West.

Pop music, in its most developed form, is an *art of war*. It represents the victory of Europe, via England, over free-market America, using the latter's own weapons. Elvis Presley and Richard Nixon were right to hate the Beatles, going so far as to wage a kind of war against John Lennon once he moved to New York with Yoko Ono.

Pop culture is an invitation to shamanism.

Three days after the release of *Sgt. Pepper's Lonely Hearts Club Band*, Jimi Hendrix opened his concert at London's Saville Theatre with a cover of the title track. In 1970, at the Isle of Wight Festival, he introduced it to the crowd this way: 'Here's the song that should replace the British National Anthem.' In a mere three days, he had time enough to buy the album, listen to it, love it, understand it, learn the title track and play it. Paul McCartney says of this event that it allowed him to grasp the impact of what they had done.

Brian Wilson, the leader of the Beach Boys, says he saw the release of *Sgt. Pepper* as a personal defeat. *Pet Sounds* was no longer and would never be 'the greatest pop album in the world'. It was nowhere near, not even close. *England had won.*

To begin with, pop invented the group. The Beatles were 'the first democratic group in the history of rock' (George Martin), a group of friends, which is tantamount to saying the first pop group.

Next, pop invented the album. Jazz, rock, as well as classical music all share, as the most developed form of the composition, the concert. But ever since *Sgt. Pepper* pop has, as its ultimate finality, the album.

The first pop group is called the Beatles.

The first pop album is called *Sgt. Pepper's Lonely Hearts Club Band*. 'They were songs that you couldn't play in concert. Songs written to be listened to on a record. That's what's important' (George Martin).

Therefore, we propose the following axiom: Pop culture is the culture that founds our time; its language is the language of the Beatles, and it's way in advance of us.

# Reviews

*Blackbird: How Black Musicians Sang the Beatles into Being*
Katie Kapurch and Jon Marc Smith
Philadelphia: University of Pennsylvania Press, 2024
ISBN: 9780271095622, 264 pp.

Most people would deny that they indulge in racist consumer practices, but in fact, few things have been more persistent than the racialization of popular music. In the twentieth century, its history is tied firmly to that of Jim Crow America, an era which coincided with the invention of electronic media such as radio and television, and it may be one of the key ways that the awful practice of segregation — 'separate but equal' (wink, wink, wink) — still has a hold over all our everyday lives.

The sad tale of how white media co-opted, exploited and whitened the work of Black artists in the 1950s and 1960s is by now well known, and unfortunately not a lot has changed since then. In the 1980s Michael Jackson — a man who felt a need to literally whiten his own skin — was one of the only Black artists played on MTV; more recently, the vexed reception of country-sounding songs by Lil Nas X and Beyoncé has proven beyond a doubt that the racial profile of individual artists is still fundamental to how popular music gets disseminated and sold.

The result of this longstanding marketing practice has been that today's listeners don't have the slightest difficulty in distinguishing the race of most singers, and can easily name music that, to them, 'sounds black' — rap, r & b, soul, Sexyy Red — as well as that which 'sounds white', that is, country music, hair metal, Taylor Swift and, most obviously, classic rock. The lines may change, but they never blur. Of course, many of the foremost performers in all those genres truly love and appreciate Black music, as evidenced by the work of Led Zeppelin and the Rolling Stones, which quite unselfconsciously committed sonic blackface by imitating blues and soul vocals, but there is still no question that they ripped it off.

But what about the Beatles? Until now, the band's beloved status has brooked little discourse regarding the tension between appropriation and appreciation that dogs most discussions around popular music. Katie Kapurch and Jon Marc Smith's new book *Blackbird: How Black Musicians Sang the Beatles into Being* takes on this difficult question, using the book to 'consider the dialog between Black musicians and the Beatles' (18). Kapurch and Smith are interested in surmising how much the Beatles, like so many bands of their era, owed to Black musical idioms and artists, and how much of their work might stand above the fray, inspiring rather than borrowing from Black pop music idioms.

This question might have been triggered in part by the section of Paul McCartney's recent (post-2018) tours in which he played the song 'Blackbird', after saying that he wrote it during the Civil Rights movement as a song of solidarity and support for those who were in it.[1] It's a truly lovely thought, and, as the authors discover, at least partially true, even if McCartney seems to have resurrected this version of it specially to fit a tour that happened during the height of the Black Lives Matter movement. Certainly, the song itself stands up to the burden of being about Civil Rights. But, as the authors also say in the introduction, 'Black Americans had songs of hope during the Civil Rights Movement [...] and "Blackbird" was not among them.' Rather, the story that has arisen around the song has allowed 'for the unfolding of layers and layers of history, especially related to Black artistry, and, as it turns out, Black music relevant to the Beatles' (10).

*Blackbird: How Black Musicians Sang the Beatles into Being* takes the position that the Beatles' music was suffused with Black idioms, ideas, images and precedents, but that it is also possible that Black artists gained much from the Beatles in return. The book begins with a discussion of how Black-African based rituals

---

1. The book refers to a concert he played in 2018 in Austin; I saw him perform it, saying the exact same introductory words, on the *Get Back* tour in 2022.

such as ring shouts, funeral parades (think *Sgt. Pepper's Lonely Hearts Club Band*), gospel, spirituals, folk and country created the genre we know as rock 'n' roll, before elaborating more fully on the connections between these things and the Beatles' *oeuvre* — of which there are many, starting with the fact that their first US releases were on a Black-owned label, Vee-Jay. The Beatles were also fans of Liverpool club owner and calypso star Lord Woodbine, as well as skiffle and r & b, and their early sets were filled with classics such as 'Twist and Shout', a song first recorded by an r & b group called the Top Notes and made popular by the Isley Brothers. And the connections don't stop there: 'Ob-La-Di, Ob-La-Da' was considered, by them at least, to be a ska song: hence, the slang use of the word 'brah', the protagonist's name Desmond, recalling Desmond Dekker; and the title phrase itself, which is Nigerian (though, the authors tell us, it might not mean exactly what we, and the Beatles, think it does).[2]

As interesting as these connections to Black vernacular musical forms are, the book is equally interested in the way that the Beatles' music was either received, or has been interpreted, by Black artists. The song 'Blackbird', for example, has been interpreted in radically different ways by radically different Black artists, including (but not limited to) Billy Preston, Sylvester, Bobby McFerrin and Bettye LaVette. The book uses these interpretations — one bluesy, one gospel-tinged, and one, McFerrin's, an *a capella* jazz version which vocalizes both lyrics and birdsong — to connect the Beatles to a host of different themes about Black music. Perhaps most important is the version done by Bettye LaVette, whose 2020 album is called *Blackbirds* in tribute to the song, because she manages to spell out the author's thesis, which, contrary to the title, is that the Beatles' work transcends race and time. At a performance at Farm Aid in 2021, LaVette said, 'This song is written by Paul McCartney, but it is about me.'[3] Both the book and this review were written before

---

2. The song gets even whiter in the hands of Orange Country ska band No Doubt, who used to finish their live shows with it; it is a B side on their big hit 'Just a Girl'.
3. At https://www.youtube.com/watch?v=qUvuCb62mJM (accessed 29 February 2024).

the March 2024 release of Beyoncé's album *Cowboy Carter*, which also includes a cover of the song 'Blackbird'. Although this version deserved a chapter to itself, at the very least it proves how timely and relevant this book's overarching theme is.

There are a number of other close readings of particular songs by Black artists over the years which the authors believe resonate closely with the Beatles, some negatively and some positively. 'Sitting on the Dock of the Bay' is interpreted here as a direct response to 'Blackbird', while Nina Simone's song 'Revolution' is interpreted as a reaction to the Beatles' song of the same title, and these are just a few of the touchstones the authors interrogate; by the end, pretty much everyone is drawn into the ring.[4] However, since the Beatles in the late 1960s were ubiquitous, it seems logical that other musicians and artists would have taken up the challenges of their music in this way.

In addition to actual versions of, and reactions to, Beatles songs, quite a lot of the book is taken up with thoughts about bird symbolism in general, especially in African mythology and in Black music as a whole. The authors show how the image of the 'Flying African' is a recurring presence in the art of the Black diaspora, evoking as they do flight from slavery. This is why (the authors suggest) birds in songs are so legion: Marley's '3 Little Birds', Leadbelly's 'Grey Goose', 'Bye, Bye, Black Bird' and many others. Indeed, they identify songs that feature a host of other yellow birds, magpies, sparrows, canaries and so on across the century, as Africans and African Americans imagine themselves flying towards freedom and home.

But could this profusion of birdsong really have anything to do with the song 'Blackbird'? Further back in time, McCartney said that the tune of 'Blackbird' was a riff on Bach's Bourée in E minor, and admitted at one point that the titular blackbird was not necessarily a bird, but a Black girl – 'We called them birds back then', he says. Nonetheless, there is no question that the song differs radically

---

[4]. Thankfully, they refrain from discussing Bill Cosby's upsetting version of 'Sergeant Pepper's Lonely Hearts Club Band', and other equally nonsensical entries, though Aretha Franklin's odd, first-person version of 'Eleanor Rigby' is parsed at length.

from, say, the Rolling Stones' now-cancelled song 'Brown Sugar', or the similarly reductive 'Sweet Black Angel', which Mick Jagger wrote about Angela Davis. It might be mere coincidence, but the Beatles 'Blackbird' *does* evoke all the same themes and incidences as the Flying African trope, when it tells its subject to 'take these broken wings and learn to fly'.

On the other hand, that line could also be seen as a summation of the one lyric that most encapsulates Paul McCartney's philosophy of life: 'Take a sad song and make it better.' In this case he has taken a sad incident in history and made it better, and also made better a story about a song that he wrote by adapting it to the times. And that's OK: as this book's profusion of material shows, the song 'Blackbird' is certainly ripe for discussion and rehabilitation. Kapurch and Smith are up for it all, even if at times the book's overall argument is overly broad and a bit anxious, falling into needless eddies of deconstruction theory, such as passages about signifyin(g) monkeys and transatlantic flows.

In truth, it's hard to see a real connection between the fact that Liverpool was a key location in the nineteenth-century slave trade and the fact that, 150 years later, the Fab Four made music there that had some connections to American Black music. Or connections between the multiplicity of songs about birds and flight in the Black African and Afro-American songbook, since birds seem to be up there with broken hearts as one of the top images in all of popular music. But despite these lapses, the specificities in this book are splendid, and make for a very fun read. Just make sure that you read it with your smart speaker nearby, so you can listen to the songs and versions of songs it mentions.

Gina Arnold<br>
University of San Francisco<br>
gina.arnold@gmail.com

***Fashioning the Beatles: The Looks that Shook the World***
Deirdre Kelly
Toronto: Sutherland House Books, 2023
ISBN: 9781990823329, 293 pp.

There was a time when the only Beatles books on many fans' shelves were titles such as Ray Coleman's *Lennon* (1985), Pete Shotton's *John Lennon: In My Life* (1983) and Peter Brown's *The Love You Make* (1983), first-hand accounts of the Beatles as a phenomenon from those within or closest to their inner circle. In the years since the group disbanded in 1970, a field of popular music studies has emerged, which in recent years has embraced and analysed the Beatles' cultural impact. Similarly, a number of key figures from the band's history such as the 'Beatle women' Cynthia Lennon, Pattie Boyd and Jenny Boyd have since written their memoirs. More recently, the highly anticipated public view into Mal Evans's diaries, Kenneth Womack's *Living the Beatles Legend: The Untold Story of Mal Evans*, was published in November 2023.

A book on the Beatles and fashion offers another window into the group. In Deirdre Kelly's *Fashioning the Beatles: The Looks that Shook the World*, the band is examined as a cultural catalyst for music and fashion during the 1960s in Britain, North America and the global beyond. Kelly's book abounds with everything from mop tops to Beatlemania wigs, the little-known story of the brown suede jacket that John Lennon wears on the cover of *Rubber Soul* (120), George Harrison and Pattie Boyd's Mary Quant wedding looks, and John Lennon and Yoko Ono's naked and monochromatic makeover period between 1968 and 1969. There is also a good introduction to Swinging London boutiques, the importance of the imported Afghan coat, and the significance of The Fool, the Dutch group who designed clothes for the band's short-lived Apple Boutique.

Given the scope of the book, a key challenge the author might face is that Beatles fans can be obsessive, and every bit of minutiae and detail needs to be accounted for. As will be seen, at times Kelly meets the mark, while at others the work falls short.

With her view of the band's Beatlemania period, the Beatles are presented as triggering 'a sea change in contemporary culture, how people viewed themselves, and how they wanted to be seen' (102) and perhaps, more stereotypically, as 'the foursome riding the winds of change' — the four horsemen of the apocalypse (102)? Early on, Kelly discusses the significance of the group's haircuts (87). It is easy to forget in our contemporary moment just how important the Beatles' unconventional masculinity was not only to rock 'n' roll but also to youth culture. The author provides a thorough discussion of their hairstyles and how the Beatles' 'mop tops' were signifiers of a new gender consciousness: 'their willingness to unselfconsciously borrow style elements from the ladies bestowed upon the Beatles an androgyny that enhanced their allure' (88). Importantly, Kelly adds that:

> The Beatles were bemused by the controversy swirling around their shaggy-haired image in the US. From their perspective, the Yanks were lucky they had come over to rescue America from being forever lost in fashion oblivion. 'When we got here you were all walking round in fucking Bermuda shorts and with Boston crewcuts and stuff on your teeth,' said John to *Rolling Stone* founder Jann Wenner. 'There was no conception of dress or any of that jazz. And we thought how hip we were.' (91)

Here, the cultural dialectic between Britain and the United States is highlighted very well: 'growing up in Liverpool, the Beatles gorged on American music and street fashion. American cultural products had inspired them as much as anything in Europe and Britain' (116). At the same time, contextual information about British culture is lacking in the discussion about *Sgt. Pepper* and the use of Victoriana in Swinging London (151). The rich tradition of pantomime, theatre, and why elements of each were incorporated into Swinging London's aesthetic is likely lost on readers who do not have the lived experience of British culture and traditions.

Published in Toronto by Sutherland House, the book has North American roots: Kelly is a Canadian writer and a noted award-winning dance critic and pop music columnist for the *Globe and Mail*. As such, some of the author's research and writing focuses on Canada, one of the first countries to feel the Beatles' global impact. Kelly cites Canadian references throughout — from fashion designer and entrepreneur Joe Mimran to the opening of Beatles boutiques in select Hudson's Bay Company stores in 1964 ('"Beatles Selection Is Better At The Bay," reads a 1964 advert highlighting the company's offering of Beatle-inspired shirts, jackets, and tailoring'; 92). It is in moments like this that Kelly's book shines. Another transatlantic connection is when Kelly highlights the OPP arm badge on McCartney's left sleeve on the *Sgt. Pepper* cover. It can be traced back to 1964, when during their stop to play two shows at Toronto's Maple Leaf Gardens, the Beatles received four Ontario Provincial Police badges as a gift while waiting to board their chartered plane for Montreal (151).

While Kelly delves into the divide between British and North American cultures, more context would help audiences not familiar with British slang (e.g., Ringo Starr's 'bum freezer' jacket is mentioned, but there is no footnote or description of the jacket itself; 48). However, the author does offer more explanation when mentioning the group's penchant for 'roll-neck (or turtleneck) sweaters' (98). Other definitions, however, appear to be incorrect. When discussing Starr's solo scene in *A Hard Day's Night*, Kelly notes that he 'slips into a rag-and-bone shop where he finds an old flat cap and dirty, formless overcoat, fashioning a disguise' (9). Technically, rag and bone men — who navigated carts, sometimes horse-drawn, through city neighbourhoods — did not have shops. Ideally the term 'junk shop' or, at best, 'antique shop' should have been used for this description.

Information provided in memoirs by Cynthia Lennon, Pattie Boyd and Jenny Boyd might have helped support a number of Kelly's points, where she effectively fills in the blanks with conjecture. One example of this is Lennon's iconic brown fur coat, which he wore from 1968 to 1969. This look is discussed on numerous occasions, yet with a little extra research the story of this item, and its contested origins, could have been explored.

Similarly, Jenny Boyd's *Jennifer Juniper: A Journey Beyond the Muse* (2021) would have assisted in the discussion about the Beatles' Apple Boutique, where Boyd, 'Pattie's younger sister, worked the floor' (179). As noted in her memoir, Boyd also assisted in the fashionable shop Passion Flower during her time living in San Francisco's Haight-Ashbury district, the epicentre of American hippie counterculture during the mid-to-late 1960s (Boyd 2020: 63). Marrying these two points with discussion of the Beatles' boutique and this brand of hippie consumerism would have illuminated the broader context in which the Beatles asserted their role as fashion muses and makers. When the Beatles decided to close their store and give the merchandise away, could it not be said that the influence of the San Francisco Diggers and their concept of 'free' — highly regarded by Derek Taylor as 'the core of the whole underground counterculture because they were our conscience' (Noble n.d.) — arrived vis-à-vis George and Pattie's visit during the Summer of Love and Jenny Boyd's time spent living and working there (Boyd 2020: 70)?

Another missed opportunity to provide important detail relevant to the book's narrative comes with its introduction of Yoko Ono, who had an immense influence on John Lennon's life and style. While Kelly does state that 'John had met the Japanese-born multidisciplinary artist, then at the vanguard of New York's conceptual art scene, in the months before the Beatles left on their prolonged search for an altered consciousness in India that year' (182), she fails to mention that Ono was already known on the London scene by the time Lennon met her at the Indica Gallery, introduced to each other by curator and gallery co-founder John Dunbar.

Kelly briefly discusses the important dynamics between photography and fashion in relation to the Beatles. A rarely seen photo of Astrid Kirchherr is a highlight of the book; however, her presence in the narrative would have benefited from further investigation. For example, she is introduced as a 'photographer's assistant' rather than a photographer in her own right. Establishing Kirchherr as an independent photographer is integral to the larger discussion of the Beatles' photo sessions with her. Moreover, it was Kirchherr, along with her friends Klaus Voormann and Jürgen Vollmer, who was responsible for moulding the band's image during their early sixties' tenure in Hamburg.

Nonetheless, there is good mention of later photo sessions, and photographers who captured the Beatles' early mop-top image, such as Michael Ward and Dezo Hoffman, but there is no inclusion or attribution of photos from those sessions. The use of Alamy for photo sources throughout the book is also concerning, as they sometimes omit important information. In other instances, proper attribution of photographs to their original photographer is missing completely (see, for example, the photo descriptions on pages 43 and 44). Understandably, establishing rights is difficult, but with this approach connections to photographers are lost (for example, the iconic John and Paul shots from David Bailey's *Box of Pin Ups* are included, but there is no mention of Bailey or these photographs' significance to Swinging London and the Beatles' image-making as a whole). Attribution is also missing from a George Harrison photo. The accompanying text states that this 'efflorescent jacket from Granny Takes a Trip that George wore to the Apple Tailoring opening became a fashion classic, immortalized in museum shows and British design retrospectives' (177). Omitted is mention that this photo was included in the *Beautiful People: The Boutique in 1960s Counterculture* exhibition at London's Fashion Textile Museum, which ran from 1 October 2021 to 13 March 2022. The photo's inclusion in the exhibition demonstrates the relevance of the Beatles and fashion in a contemporary context, in relation to boutique culture and independent designers in Swinging London in the 1960s, so mentioning it would have highlighted the band's continuing influence on this aspect of cultural life.

Another issue with attribution is the lack of citations for chapter heading quotes such as George Harrison saying that the Beatles were responsible for 'selling all that corduroy and making it swing' in the mid-sixties. This quote is taken from *The Beatles Anthology* (1995) but would be lost on any reader not familiar with the ins and outs of the documentary and/or its accompanying book. Conversely, Kelly makes a fantastic job of discussing the history and significance of the British designers and Swinging London boutiques that 'sold all that corduroy' by highlighting their relationship to youth culture, fashion and the Beatles. Similarly, Harrison's well-known quip upon first meeting George Martin — 'I don't like your tie' — is missing the concluding 'for a start', which would have emphasized Harrison's countercultural defiance of the older Martin (46).

Overall, there are many strong points and claims made throughout the text. For example, it is fascinating to learn that Pattie Boyd designed the striking lavender-suede gladiator sandals that she wore during her ill-fated visit to San Franciso's Haight-Ashbury district with Harrison (162). But where did Kelly get this information? Dates, addresses and locations could be better specified at times as well: the Apple Boutique was nearer Regent's Park than Oxford Street, as the author suggests. Also, the Beatles' 'packed party' for the Apple Boutique's official opening needs a more specific date (7 December 1967). Such details would better set out the Beatles' chronology as related to their fashion forays.

A challenge with Kelly's book is that its intended audience is never clear. While it's not an academic book, is it meant for academics looking for research material about the Beatles and fashion, or is it solely meant for a more general readership? Facts are presented and sources used, but what is missing is further insight from the author on the many points of discussion included in the text. Ringo Starr wore a Mr Fish shirt for his *White Album* portrait, yes, but so what? Why? The Beatles were a stylish group and they 'changed everything', as stated in the quote from Nik Cohn in the book's pre-preface, but were they truly at the vanguard of fashion or was it simply their role as high-profile musicians that helped them to set fashion trends? Were they simply vehicles for the era's changing fashions? Kelly also makes links between the group's influence and the modern context:

> Before the Beatles, no other rock group had entered so aggressively, and with such fanfare, the rapidly evolving world of fashion retail. The Apple Boutique was the prototype for the cross-branding of music and fashion that the likes of Beyoncé, Diddy, Rhianna, Kanye West, Drake, Justin Bieber, Jennifer Lopez, and Victoria Beckham, to name but a handful of contemporary pop stars with their own global fashion brands, have made a standard business model today. (176)

Is this the case? Fashion is an important part of the Beatles' cultural impact but this comparison to modern-day celebrities runs counter to the anti-commercial ethos attached to the Beatles as counter-culture figures, who, in the end, gave away their Apple clothes and merchandise for free. What we have here is a compendium of facts and an overview of Beatles fashion that will interest Beatles fans from a reportage perspective, with information from other sources brought together into one, new text.

Marlie Centawer
Liverpool John Moores University
marliecentawer@icloud.com

## Bibliography

Boyd, Jenny (2020) *Jennifer Juniper: A Journey Beyond the Muse* (London: Urbane).
Brown, Pete (1983) *The Love You Make: An Insider's Story of the Beatles* (London: Macmillan).
Coleman, Ray (1985) *Lennon: The Definitive Biography* (New York: McGraw-Hill).
Junor, Penny and Pattie Boyd (2007) *Wonderful Tonight: George Harrison, Eric Clapton and Me* (London: Headline Review).
Lennon, Cynthia (2005) *John* (London: Hodder and Stoughton).
Noble, Eric (n.d.) The Digger Archives: It Was Twenty Years Ago Today, https://www.diggers.org/it_was_twenty.htm (accessed December 2023).
Schaffner, Nicholas and Pete Shotton (1983) *John Lennon: In My Life* (New York: Stein and Day).
Womack, Kenneth (2023) *Living the Beatles Legend: The Untold Story of Mal Evans* (New York: Dey Street Books).
Wonfor, Geoff (dir.) (1995) *The Beatles Anthology*.

*Living the Beatles Legend: On the Road with the Fab Four — The Mal Evans Story*
Kenneth Womack
London: Mudlark/HarperCollins, 2023
ISBN: 9780008551216, 592 pp.

*Living the Beatles Legend: On the Road with the Fab Four — The Mal Evans Story* (published in North America with the subtitle *The Untold Story of Mal Evans*) by the American Beatles scholar Kenneth Womack will almost certainly be the last insider account of the band, as their era approaches the edge of living memory and everyone from their chauffeur onwards has long since had their say. As this book attests, using its subject's own unpublished words and photographs, Mal Evans was a true believer from the Cavern onwards, witness to all the key moments, and is clearly part of the Beatles' scenius group. Womack's work is especially timely, since Mal Evans recently came to life for a new audience in Peter Jackson's *The Beatles: Get Back*, in which he appears as the uber-genial Beatles' confidant, lyric scribe, caterer, fixer and anvil obtainer, etc. etc. What *Get Back* (understandably) doesn't show are Evans's roles as the band's drug purchaser and transporter, sexual procurer, housekeeper, lightning rod for bad temper and bouncer, all of which Womack touches on to a greater or lesser degree. What emerges in *Living the Beatles Legend* is a moving but troubling account of Evans's life and work in which his indefatigable dedication is only matched by ongoing insecurity about his position, his thrill at proximity to fame seesawing with the damage his unpredictable chosen life did to his own family and personal well-being.

*Living the Beatles Legend* is underwritten by the exclusive access the author was granted to Evans's diaries, personal archive and the manuscript of his unpublished autobiographies as source materials. These had been put into storage by their intended publisher in New York when Lily, Evans's wife, blocked publication of the autobiography after his death in 1976. There is a touching foreword by Gary, Evans's son, and Womack is effusive in his acknowledgement of the family and of Yoko Ono, whose help was instrumental in saving these materials from being thrown out and returned to the family. Such odd circumstances create complications for the project as well as advantages. While this is not an authorized biography, it occupies the same slightly (but significantly) ambiguous area that Richard Morton Jack's excellent biography of Nick Drake does, wherein generous family support, though sincere and non-editorializing, must have had a psychologically inhibiting effect on the writer, however unintentional. Judgements or critical contextualizations of questionable or damaging behaviour are few and far between here. Indeed, Womack is writing from the ironic position of having a scoop in terms of primary sources, but then creating a biography that necessarily displaces Evans's own unpublished autobiographies, without which he could not have completed this project. Moreover, Womack (and Evans himself) evidently realize what a slippery genre the diary is, how such apparently off-the-cuff private writing always has an eye on posterity, either the writer's future self or some other, as yet unknown, reader. That said, since so much of Womack's narrative depends on Evans's writing and as this book exists to see events from his point of view, the primary sources might occasionally be taken a little too much at face value. The upsides to this heavy reliance on a few new sources are in those moments where Evans's quoted writing has the sheen of wet ink, which feels miraculous in the knowing, supersaturated Beatles world of 2024.

A question that must be asked of any new book about the Beatles is brutally existential: is this really necessary? Put another way, does it have enough unseen material or a previously unconsidered angle such that its publication is worthwhile? In this case, while the main sequence of events is entirely familiar, there is a stream of fascinating new details to nuance the narrative and justify the project. I did not know that it was Evans who stood up to Brian Epstein in Cincinnati to prevent the band from being electrocuted when they were due to go on in a rainstorm. Nor was I aware of the incident when Evans was vehement with the Beatles in his opinion that anti-Vietnam war protestors should be shot by the authorities (as they were at Kent State). If these details seem like scraps to some, it is worth recognizing that it is hard to predict what information will be most valued by future generations of scholars, and that there are now few witnesses to the 1960s who are not dead or talked out. Recording every detail (or myth, or lie, or piece of gossip) about figures of such enduring cultural importance as the Beatles is key before these are lost forever. Jarvis Cocker was wrong to mock the inclusion of Lennon's shopping lists in Hunter Davies's edition of *The John Lennon Letters*, because this apparently worthless trivia actually gives a telling glimpse into the domestic life that Lennon prioritized over music making for a while, and also records the cross-cultural adjustments he had to make while living in the US.

Womack has done posterity a service by his comprehensive approach to delivering the story, and his book is aimed appropriately at a general audience. The writing is limpid and the text is chunked into short sections with amusing titles, but a little more pizzazz in the prose would add life, especially to a work about such verbally witty people. The many unfamiliar or unpublished photographs and graphics are well chosen and some background is sketched in to orient the less Beatle-obsessive reader, sometimes from other secondary sources and new interviews. That said, even at a gargantuan five hundred pages, *Living the Beatles Legend* seems light on analysis, rarely moving from the narrative mode, where more explicit interpretative and argumentative framing of the sources might produce a better power to weight ratio.

What do we learn about Evans and so about the band? Womack generally lets Evans speak for himself as far as possible, quoting and paraphrasing to capture his voice and attitudes, and his subject comes across as a tortured individual who could not reconcile his globalized lifestyle with the commitments he had made pre-Beatles (his marriage and family expectations). The moment when his hero, Elvis Presley, telephones him at his modest family home in England to wish him a happy Easter typifies the cultural and spatial incongruities he had to span, some thrilling, some disturbing. The expectation that he would use a cellophane wrapping machine to package drugs which he then carried across borders, for instance, encapsulates the sense that he embodies the maxim 'be careful what you wish for'. One especially telling moment is when McCartney says to Evans: 'You are my servant. You do as you are told.' (So much for hippy egalitarianism.) Devastated by this blunt declaration of hierarchy, Evans went to see Lennon, who misquoted Milton's sonnet 26, saying 'They also lead who serve.' This literary finessing of the original insult pacified Evans, but changed nothing, and he seems to have been underpaid for many years.

Despite all this, Evans carefully balanced the needs and sometimes rivalrous desire for attention of all four Beatles, and this book is suitably even handed to them all. All four appear as contradictory and changeable, as young people under pressure are, and occasionally comically immature, such as when George Harrison has a tantrum when his artfully faded denim jacket is pinched from the Magical Mystery Tour bus. Another plus is the recounting of Evans's own creativity, given much more coverage here than in any previous work. Beyond his well-known small contributions to recordings, it seems highly likely that he co-authored the lyrics to 'Sgt. Pepper's Lonely Hearts Club Band' and 'Fixing a Hole', but was never credited, even in terms of off-the-record royalties (literally and figuratively). This careless treatment of Evans financially indicates the way he could never transcend his designated work identity. Yet to some degree Evans is beloved precisely because he was an everyman, functioning as a fan placeholder to generations of Beatlemaniacs who have identified with him as a relatable visible point within the blinding constellation of genius.

While *Living the Beatles Legend* is rightly concerned with seeing Evans and the band in their era, it inevitably raises questions about what new generations of fans will make of the story over time, especially now that AI has given the band a virtual lease of life with the release of 'Now and Then'. For instance, some of my undergraduate students interpreted *Get Back* as a documentary about workplace bullying with regard to the treatment of George Harrison before his resignation. This apparent category mistake has some justification on reflection: think, for example, of Lennon patting Harrison's head after hearing him demo 'I Me Mine', before noting patronizingly that the Beatles don't do waltzes. (This interaction puts a very different spin on his waltzing Yoko around the studio shortly afterwards, a moment usually seen as charming but which is actually extremely passive aggressive.)

It seems likely that new generations of Beatles listeners will ask more searching questions of the band, some of which might be utterly anachronistic, others valid then or legitimate in the life of the music and story going forwards. The mixed treatment of Evans and his family detailed in *Living the Beatles Legend* shows the band to have acted in ways that are sometimes belatedly sensitive (as late as the 1980s Harrison visited Lily, then widowed, to apologize for introducing Evans to the woman he left her for), sometimes dehumanizing (Lennon called his cat 'Mal'). None of this will go down well in future, when fans approach the band via arbitrary streaming of the music rather than the crafted teleology of legend. More troublingly still, Womack supplies fresh information on the sexual/emotional exploitation of young, sometimes underage fans (and their mothers), including evidence of Evans using his position for this purpose. This topic is now rightly getting serious attention from scholars, journalists, podcasters and fans. Younger people among these groups (and others) have little patience with the 'different times' gloss on such behaviour that has been touted in the past, and there is clearly much more to say in future analyses of male group dynamics, based on the fresh testimony here.

Womack reveals that there will be a companion volume to this book which will give access to some of the raw materials he based his work on. How comprehensive this second helping will be in terms of facsimile reproduction versus transcription remains to be seen, but it is likely that it will be a reasonably priced volume rather than a Genesis Publications-style extravaganza that is out of reach for most. This is a welcome and refreshing stance versus the hoarding or gatekeeping mentality that sometimes prevails in collecting and scholarly circles. The chance to view the archive will add another layer to our understanding of Evans and the quotidian Beatles world he inhabited, as the reproduced diary pages that are included in the present book make manifest the content of the form. Two examples: 1) the captionless cartoon of a livid Paul McCartney looking a bit like Fred Flintstone, when clearly the words exchanged that day had been too painful to record; and 2) Evans's own fond sketch of his four colleagues walking over the zebra crossing for the *Abbey Road* photo shoot, above which he describes going to Regent's Park Zoo later that day with Harrison to wander and meditate in the sun, somehow unrecognized by the public: a lovely inkling of the off hours usually obscured from sight.

In short, this is an interesting read, put together with sensitivity and careful scholarship. Womack cannily reuses Evans's own title for the putative autobiography and honours a subject who, for all his flaws, deserves understanding and recognition. Philip Larkin famously noted, 'When you get to the top, there is nowhere to go but down. But the Beatles could not get down.' As a not-quite-Beatle, Mal Evans fell vertiginously in the aftermath, as Womack relates here, and he remains a fascinating figure who will enjoy further attention when the second volume of primary sources comes out. They could not have done what they did without him.

Christian Lloyd
Queen's University, Canada
christian.lloyd@queensu.ca

## Bibliography

Cocker, Jarvis. (2012) 'The John Lennon Letters, edited by Hunter Davies – review', The Guardian, https://www.theguardian.com/books/2012/oct/10/john-lennon-letters-hunter-davies-review (accessed 19 April 2024).

*The Beatles in Perspective: A Carnival of Light*
**Edited by James McGrath and Peter Mills**
Sheffield: Equinox, 2023
ISBN: 9781800502420, 274 pp.

In their introduction to *The Beatles in Perspective: A Carnival of Light*, the editors, James McGrath and Peter Mills, begin by posing an often asked question: 'Does the world need another book on the Beatles?' Judging by the diverse reflections, refractions and perspectives opened up within this prismatic collection of essays, the answer is a resounding 'Yes'. The introduction itself raises further, more interesting questions about what Beatles Studies actually is, but allows the various contributions to respond for themselves through adding to and reinforcing an ever-expanding discipline at the same time as they shed new light and colour. The book is divided into three distinct parts dealing with the cultural and historical contexts of the Beatles, the wide and sometimes disturbing spectrum of fandom, and a final section that ranges more widely into less well-known territory than the first two parts suggest. Having said that, while such structuring is useful in helping readers to navigate their way through the book, all the essays are interconnected and coalesce to extend the boundaries of Beatles Studies by giving an often original twist to something previously familiar.

The first section of the book — 'Culture and History' — kicks off with co-editor James McGrath revisiting the Beatles' relationship to working-class identity together with their often overlooked exposure to Black culture and music in Liverpool, both of which resonated throughout their work. He brings peripheral figures from the Beatles' 'pre-history' — such as Vinnie Tow and Lord Woodbine (Harold Phillips) — into the critical spotlight for present and future consideration, and offers interesting readings of, for example, 'Ob-La-Di, Ob-La-Da' and 'Get Back' to reveal their sociopolitical relevance in the context of late 1960s Britain. McGrath's astute observations on class and race are followed by an interview with Mark Christian, who also insists on the importance of future Beatles scholarship looking in more detail at the impact of African-American artists, particularly in the early days of the band, something that Richard Mills's soon-to-be-published book *The Beatles and Black Music: Post-Colonial Theory, Musicology and Remix Culture* (2024) will no doubt address.

Postcolonial theory, in particular Edward Said's reflections on 'Orientalism', concerns Sharif Gemie in a rereading of 'Tomorrow Never Knows' that posits the idea that John Lennon misread Tibetan culture through naively taking on board Timothy Leary's *The Psychedelic Experience* as an authoritative guide to its religious principles and practices. Gemie understands the song to be an example of Said's observation of the ways in which the West has a tendency to reinvent the East by mistakenly appropriating it, even if the motives are based on 'an admiration or even an affection' (56). These blind spots have often, so he argues, manifested themselves in critical readings of 'Tomorrow Never Knows', and Gemie works to correct the vision of writers such as Ian MacDonald who offer — so he believes — an equally naive interpretation of the track.

Thinking more about the Beatles in the context of Western culture, Jon Goss focuses on the childish playfulness and hyperactive movement of the Beatles that, he suggests, allowed them to occupy a space where they could resist the atrophying characteristics of the older generation and the Establishment. Even if such kinetic creativity was ultimately compromised by global success and the youthful freedoms that they found inevitably temporal, Goss argues that they constructed a utopia that can still be glimpsed in their music and films, but for all the clues provided through his fascinating reflections on the Beatles' legacy, he is tantalizingly vague about what we are supposed to do with that (if anything). History and culture are equally well served in Colin Campbell's conclusion to the first part of the book which explores how the Beatles regarded themselves as artists from the outset and how, for example, their interest and association with the lifestyle and ideology of the Beats, or their coming into contact with European existentialism, helped to affirm the artistic tendencies that manifested themselves progressively throughout their work and in turn shaped the world around them.

In the second part of the collection — 'Audience, Fanhood, Interpretation' — Stephanie Fremaux begins by considering the changes that have taken place in being a Beatles fan both during the 1960s and beyond. She looks at the ways in which more recent fans interact on a new and more equal footing with their idols through social media, video games, exhibitions and internet concert experiences, and how these forms of experience allow individuals and groups to express their fandom in a more active and engaged manner that allows them to participate directly in maintaining the Beatles' legacy in the evolving digital age. Richard Mills is similarly interested in the empowerment that fans experience as a result of new technologies and the ability to create and recreate the Beatles, to access and appropriate them, that the internet facilitates. Mills offers a useful and thorough introduction to thinking about the evolution of fandom, and his fear of creating anything canonical or orthodox is deflected by the variety of fan activity that is explored and celebrated: early forms of fandom in the 1960s, Beatles conventions, the problematics of journalists as fans, slash fiction, tribute bands, fan activity on YouTube, obsessional forms of fandom — all are carefully examined as manifestations of a participatory and transformative culture. Picking up from Mills, Mike Kirkup takes a well-researched look at *The Beatles Book/Beatles Monthly* and its association with Beatles fandom as it unfolded in the 1960s. He sees it as an interesting testimony to the ways in which many fans struggled to adapt to the Beatles' swift and sometimes radical change of musical and stylistic direction, and how, as well as creating a sense of intimacy between 'the Boys' and their followers, it also provided a space where concerns, complaints and criticisms could be posted on a physical, printed letters page. Showing how fans responded in real time as it were, without the hindsight, history and technology that today's fans have access to, Kirkup's chapter allows for a refreshing view of early, original responses to the Beatles that encourages us, so he argues, to reflect more deeply on the evolution of fandom and the differences and similarities between 'now and then'.

Gerry Carlin and Mark Jones turn their full attention to the dark side of fandom in thinking about how the open-ended nature of the Beatles' lyrics led to Charles Manson's psychotic reading of the *White Album*, but they also call out critics and rock journalists who have viewed an inherent nihilism and violence at the heart of that record. They question such readings, but acknowledge the ways in which the album's association with Manson has had an undoubted and sometimes toxic influence through remaining 'the dominant cultural interpretation' (195). Not for the first time in the book, Ian MacDonald comes in for particular flak, but perhaps they go too far in suggesting that he has an overriding tendency to read the *White Album* through Manson's eyes. Like the disastrous Altamont Speedway Free Festival, Carlin and Jones see the *White Album* and Manson's 'tragic misunderstanding' of it (198) as inextricably bound up with the traumatic loss of the sixties utopian dream, and in this sense, perhaps, they are not so far removed from MacDonald's point of view, even though they raise some valid questions about certain aspects of *Revolution in the Head* and Beatles criticism generally.

The final part of the critical carnival — 'Savoy Truffles: Further Perspectives' — finds us first sharing in Martin Malone's quest to find the origin and location of a small black and white photograph of Paul McCartney taken some time in early 1963 while the Beatles were on a short tour of Scotland. Perhaps of greater interest than the detective work and archival research employed are Malone's reflections on the photograph as a significant moment captured between the release of 'Love Me Do' and the very soon to be rapid escalation towards national celebrity: a moment between innocence and experience also sensed in the chapter's more general reflections on a tour during which the Beatles played to about twenty people at the Dingwall Town Hall. In bringing the photograph to light, Malone offers an exercise in both the experience of hands-on archival Beatles research together with a poet's sensibility towards the 'spots of time' that mark the history of the band and the wider culture that they influenced and were a part of.[5] Ed Prideaux concludes with a fascinating look at the brief history of one of the first US bandwagon-jumping groups caught up in a scam that saw them contracted to tour Argentina in 1964 by an unscrupulous agent who promoted them as the Beatles proper. Paradoxically, while there was much anger and disappointment, the American Beetles generated a media storm replicating that which surrounded the real Beatles in other parts of the world. Prideaux notes how articles in the Argentinian press reacted to the Beetles in ways that echoed — sometimes in a more extreme

---

5. In Book XI of *The Prelude* (1805), Wordsworth refers to significant moments that mark and influence one's existence as 'spots of time'.

manner than in coverage of the originals — concerns about, for example, their gender and sexuality or whether they were any good as musicians. The Beatles — with an A — never played in Argentina, but Prideaux shows how the American Beetles, through an act of unofficial proxy, gave it a taste of the mania and controversy that eventually inspired more considered media reaction to the global and local impact of the 'English Beatles' and played a part in cementing John, Paul, George and Ringo as important cultural agents in South America to this day.

The tripartite structure of the *The Beatles in Perspective* is also marked and generously filled by three informal, but informative, interviews between the editors and the veteran of American Beatles scholarship, Russell Reising. In the first of these interludes, they discuss the longevity of the Beatles and how their defiance of generic appropriation gives them a timeless quality that might account for their enduring popularity. This is followed by a discussion about the ongoing and now trans-generational appeal of the Beatles, their dedication to the creation of ever richer soundscapes and the influence of the avant-garde. They also discuss the early Beatles as an important conduit for the popularity of Motown in the UK, but the best is saved until last. After more banter between the editors and Reising, we are treated to some humorous tales about Tony Sheridan and Allan Williams before the conversation turns to thoughts about the style, subjects and title of the book we have just read. All of which ends *The Beatles in Perspective: Carnival of Light* in a self-reflexive manner, prompting the reader to think about the themes explored throughout and how the chapters stand up on their own and yet are enriched by the completeness of the whole, rather like the songs of the Beatles themselves.

My only grumble about what is a welcome addition to Equinox's 'Studies in Popular Music' series concerns the fact that most of the contributors are blokes, and it would have been interesting to have had some feminist or LGBTQ+ approaches to add to the choice of flavours alongside the Savoy Truffle and the other rich delicacies proposed. Nonetheless, the interdisciplinary nature of a volume made up of well-known and newer voices, together with the wide range of subjects explored and theoretical angles applied, makes for a text that is a very sound contribution to an ever-growing critical corpus.

Ben Winsworth
University of Orleans, France
ben.winsworth@univ-orleans.fr

## Bibliography

Mills, Richard (2024) *The Beatles and Black Music: Post-Colonial Theory, Musicology and Remix Culture* (London: Bloomsbury Academic).
Wordsworth, William (2008) *The Major Works* (Oxford: Oxford University Press).

Printed and bound by CPI Group (UK) Ltd, Croydon, CR0 4YY
06/04/2026

14854957-0001